Routledge
Taylor & Francis Group
NEW YORK AND LONDON

INSTRUCTIONS FOR CONTRIBUTORS

Applied Measurement in Education, sponsored by the Oscar and Luella Buros Center for Testing, is a scholarly journal dedicated to the application of educational and psychological measurement research to the educational process. Its intended audience consists of researchers and practitioners who are interested in research likely to have an impact on educational measurement practice. A major aim of the journal is to provide both a greater understanding of educational measurement issues and an improved use of measurement techniques in education.

Types of manuscripts that will be considered for publication in *Applied Measurement in Education* include (a) reports of original applied research focusing on measurement issues in educational contexts, (b) presentations of innovative strategies for solving existing educational measurement problems, and (c) integrative reviews of research pertaining to contemporary measurement issues. An additional section of the journal will be dedicated to providing comparative reviews of tests and methods currently used in addressing specific educational measurement needs. The editors also welcome proposals for special issues dealing with a focused treatment of a particular area of applied educational measurement.

Manuscript Submission: Submit four manuscript copies to *Applied Measurement in Education,* 21 Teachers College Hall, University of Nebraska–Lincoln, Lincoln, NE 68588–0352. Only original manuscripts submitted to *Applied Measurement in Education* will be considered for publication. The cover letter should include a statement that the manuscript is not being simultaneously submitted elsewhere. Manuscripts will not be returned.

Format and Organization: Manuscripts should be prepared according to the guidelines in the *Publication Manual of the American Psychological Association* (5th ed.). Double-space all text. On the first page, indicate the title of the manuscript, the names and affiliations of authors, and the name and address of the person to whom reprint requests are to be sent; suggest a shortened version of the title of the manuscript for use as a running head (40 characters or fewer, including spaces). On the second page, provide a 100- to 175-word abstract. On the third page (the first text page), type the title of the manuscript.

Permissions: Authors are responsible for all statements made in their work and for obtaining permission from copyright owners to use a lengthy quotation (500 words or more) or to reprint or adapt a table or figure published elsewhere. Authors should write to both author(s) and publisher of such material to request nonexclusive world rights in all languages for use in the article and in future editions of it.

Content: Do not use new technical words, psychological jargon or slang, or terminology not consistent with the style guidelines in the *Publication Manual of the APA.* Define any abbreviations or acronyms the first time they are used.

Figures and Tables: All figures and tables should be numbered separately using Arabic numerals and should be grouped at the end of the manuscript. Clearly visible notes within the text should indicate approximate placement of figures and tables. Figures must be professionally prepared and must be camera-ready. Type figure captions on a separate sheet. Write the article title and figure number lightly in pencil on the back of each piece of artwork. Refer to the *Publication Manual of the APA* for format of tables. Double-space.

References: Double-space. Compile references alphabetically (see the *Publication Manual of the APA* for multiple-author citations and references). Spell out names of journals. Provide page numbers of chapters in edited books. Text citations must correspond accurately to the references in the reference list.

Page Proofs: Authors are sent page proofs of their manuscripts and are asked to proofread them for printer's errors and other defects. Correction of typographical errors will be made without charge; other alterations will be charged to the author.

Applied Measurement in Education is published quarterly by Lawrence Erlbaum Associates, Inc., 10 Industrial Avenue, Mahwah, NJ 07430–2262. Subscriptions for Volume 15, 2002 are available only on a calendar-year basis. **Printed** journal subscription rates for Volume 15, 2002 are $50 for individuals and $395 for institutions within the United States and Canada; $80 for individuals and $425 for institutions outside the United States and Canada. Order printed subscriptions through the Journal Subscription Department, Lawrence Erlbaum Associates, Inc., 10 Industrial Avenue, Mahwah, NJ 07430–2262. Full price print subscribers to Volume 15, 2002 are entitled to receive the **electronic** version free of charge. *Electronic-only* subscriptions are also available at a reduced price of $45 for individuals and $355.50 for institutions.

Address changes should include the mailing label or a facsimile. Claims for missing issues cannot be honored beyond 4 months after mailing date. Duplicate copies cannot be sent to replace issues not delivered due to failure to notify publisher of change of address.

This journal is abstracted or indexed in *PsycINFO/Psychological Abstracts; Contents Pages in Education; ISA; ISI: Current Contents/Social & Behavioral Sciences, Social Sciences Citation Index, Research Alert, Social SciSearch; Social Research Methodology; Education Index; Education Abstracts;* EBSCO*host* Products.

Microform copies of this journal are available through ProQuest Information and Learning, P.O. Box 1346, Ann Arbor, MI 48106–1346. For more information, call 1-800-521-0600, extension 2888.

First published by Lawrence Erlbaum Associates, Inc., Publishers
10 Industrial Avenue
Mahwah, NJ 07430

This edition published 2013 by Routledge

Routledge
711 Third Avenue
New York
NY 10017

Routledge
2 Park Square, Milton Park
Abingdon
Oxon, OX14 4RN

Routledge is an imprint of the Taylor & Francis Group, an informa business

APPLIED MEASUREMENT IN EDUCATION, *15*(4), 335–336
Copyright © 2002, Lawrence Erlbaum Associates, Inc.

GUEST EDITOR'S NOTE

ADVANCES IN COMPUTERIZED SCORING OF COMPLEX ITEM FORMATS

In 1936, Hartog and Rhodes (1936) documented the limitations of scoring essays. The overwhelming evidence was that in practical high-stakes settings, the reliability of expert ratings was unacceptably low. With the introduction of automated scoring procedures for multiple-choice items, the combination of lower reliability and relative inefficiency made constructed-response items all but obsolete.

Not surprisingly, with the increasing interest in performance assessment during recent years, critics have returned to these same arguments (e.g., Wainer & Thissen, 1993). Wainer and Thissen graphically demonstrated the difference in efficiency for fixed-format and constructed-response items in terms of the difference in scoring costs for these formats. However, more recent developments have been made in the practical application of computer-automated scoring systems, which may improve both the efficiency and reliability of scoring for constructed-response items. These procedures are being used in large-scale and high-stakes testing. Registration for architects as well as licensure for physicians requires passing a test that includes complex constructed-response items delivered and scored by computer. Similarly, computerized scoring of essays is now a routine part of admissions and placement testing.

The move from research to operations for computerized delivery and scoring of complex constructed-response items was the motivation for this special issue. The four articles presented here are intended to provide an overview of the state of the art for such applications. The issue begins with an overview by Zenisky and Sireci describing the range of computer-delivered formats and computerized scoring systems that are currently in use. The authors of the remaining articles provide three views of validity in the context of computer-delivered and scored assessments. In their article, Mislevy, Steinberg, Breyer, Almond, and Johnson present an evidence-centered approach to the design and analysis of complex assessments. The presentation is made in the context of a specific assessment project but provides an example of how both tasks and scoring systems can be developed to support the production of interpretable scores. The articles by Yang, Buckendahl, Juszkiewicz, and Bhola and by Clauser, Kane, and Swanson provide two additional and contrasting discussions of the validity argument for test scores produced by computer-automated scoring systems. Although the three validity-oriented articles presented in this issue provide contrasting views, they are not (for the most part) contradictory.

It is hoped that together these four articles provide the reader with both an appreciation of the state of the art for computer-automated scoring systems and a perspective on the issues that must be considered and the evidence that must be collected to produce automated scoring systems that allow for valid inference.

Brian E. Clauser
National Board of Medical Examiners
Philadelphia, PA
Guest Editor

REFERENCES

Hartog, P., & Rhodes, E. C. (1936). *The marks of examiners.* London: MacMillan.
Wainer, H., & Thissen, D. (1993). Combining multiple-choice and constructed-response test scores: Toward a Marxist theory of test construction. *Applied Measurement in Education, 6,* 103–118.

APPLIED MEASUREMENT IN EDUCATION, *15*(4), 337–362

Technological Innovations in Large-Scale Assessment

April L. Zenisky and Stephen G. Sireci

Center for Educational Assessment, School of Education
University of Massachusetts Amherst

Computers have had a tremendous impact on assessment practices over the past half century. Advances in computer technology have substantially influenced the ways in which tests are made, administered, scored, and reported to examinees. These changes are particularly evident in computer-based testing, where the use of computers has allowed test developers to re-envision what test items look like and how they are scored. By integrating technology into assessments, it is increasingly possible to create test items that can sample as broad or as narrow a range of behaviors as needed while preserving a great deal of fidelity to the construct of interest. In this article we review and illustrate some of the current technological developments in computer-based testing, focusing on novel item formats and automated scoring methodologies. Our review indicates that a number of technological innovations in performance assessment are increasingly being researched and implemented by testing programs. In some cases, complex psychometric and operational issues have successfully been dealt with, but a variety of substantial measurement concerns associated with novel item types and other technological aspects impede more widespread use. Given emerging research, however, there appears to be vast potential for expanding the use of more computerized constructed-response type items in a variety of testing contexts.

The rapid evolution of computers and computing technology has played a critical role in defining current measurement practices. Many tests are now administered on a computer, and a number of psychometric software programs are widely used to facilitate all aspects of test development and analysis. Such technological advances provide testing programs with many new tools with which to build tests and understand assessment data from a variety of perspectives and traditions. The po-

---

Requests for reprints should be sent to April L. Zenisky, School of Education, 156 Hills South, University of Massachusetts, Amherst, MA 01003–4140. E-mail: azenisky@educ.umass.edu

tential for computers to influence testing is not yet exhausted, however, as the needs and interests of testing programs continue to evolve.

Test users increasingly express interest in assessing skills that can be difficult to fully tap using traditional paper-and-pencil tests. As the potential for integrating technology into task presentation and response collection has become more of a practical reality, a variety of innovative computerized constructed-response item types emerge. Many of these new types call for reconceptualization of what examinee responses look like, how they are entered into the computer, and how they are scored (Bennett, 1998). This is good news for test users in all testing contexts, as a greater selection of item types may allow test developers to increase the extent to which tasks on a test approximate the knowledge, skills, and abilities of interest.

The purpose of this article is to review the current advances in computer-based assessment, including innovative item types, response technologies, and scoring methodologies. Each of these topics defines an area where applications of technology are rapidly evolving. As research and practical implementation continues, these emerging assessment methods are likely to significantly alter measurement practices. In this article we provide an overview of the recent developments in task presentation and response scoring algorithms that are currently used or have the potential for use in large-scale testing.

INNOVATIONS IN TASK PRESENTATION

Response Actions

In developing test items for computerized performance assessment, one critical component for test developers to think about is the format of the response an examinee is to provide. It may at first seem backward to think about examinee response formats before item stems, but how answers to test questions are structured has an obvious bearing on the nature of the information being collected. Thus, as the process of designing assessment tasks gets underway, some reflection on the inferences to be made on the basis of test scores and how best to collect that data is essential.

To this end, an understanding of what Parshall, Davey, and Pashley (2000) termed *response action* and what Bennett, Morley and Quardt (2000) described as *response type* may be helpful. Prior to actually constructing test items, some consideration of the type of responses desired from examinees and the method by which the responses could be entered can help a test developer to discern the kinds of item types that might provide the most useful and construct-relevant information about an examinee (Mislevy, Steinberg, Breyer, Almond, & Johnson, 1999). In a computer-based testing (CBT) environment, the precise nature of the information that test developers would like examinees to provide might be best expressed in one of several ways. For example, examinees could be required to type text-based responses, enter numerical answers via a keyboard or by clicking onscreen buttons, or manipulate or synthesize information on a computer screen in some way (e.g., use a mouse to direct an onscreen cursor to click on text boxes, pull-down menus, or audio or video prompts). The mouse can also be used to draw onscreen images as well as to "drag-and-drop" objects.

The keyboard and mouse are the input devices most familiar to examinees and are the ones overwhelmingly implemented in current computerized testing applications, but response actions in a computerized context are not exclusively limited to the keyboard and mouse. Pending additional research, some additional input devices by which examinees' constructed responses could one day be collected include touch screens, light pens, joysticks, trackballs, speech recognition software and microphones, and pressure-feedback (haptic) devices (Parshall, Davey, & Pashley, 2000). Each of these emerging methods represent inventive ways by which test developers and users can gather different pieces of information about examinee skills. However, at this time these alternate data collection mechanisms are largely in experimental stages and are not yet implemented as part of many (if any) novel item types. For this reason, we focus on emerging item types that use the keyboard, mouse, or both for collecting responses from examinees.

Novel Item Types

For many testing programs, the familiar item types currently in use such as multiple-choice and essay items provide sufficient measurement information for the kinds of decisions being made on the basis of test scores. However, a substantial number of increasingly interactive item types that may increase measurement information are now available, and some are being used operationally. This proliferation of item types has largely come about in response to requests from test consumers for assessments aligned more closely with the constructs or skills being assessed. Although many of these newer item types were developed for specific testing applications such as licensure, certification, or graduate admissions testing, it is possible to envision each of these item types being adapted in countless ways to access different constructs as needed by a particular testing program.

Numerous computerized item types have emerged over the past decade, so it is virtually impossible to illustrate and describe them all in a single article. Nevertheless, we conducted a review of the psychometric literature and of test publishers' Web sites and selected several promising item types for presentation and discussion. A nonexhaustive list of 21 of these item types is presented in Table 1, along with a brief description of each type and some relevant references. Some of the item types listed in Table 1 are being used operationally, whereas others have been only proposed for use.

TABLE 1
Computerized Performance Assessment Item Types

Item Format	Brief Description	Selected Citation(s)
Drag-and-drop (select-and-place)	Given scenario or problem, examinees click and drag an object to the center of the appropriate answer field (see Figure 1).	Fitzgerald (2001); Luecht (2001); Microsoft Corporation (1998)
Graphical modeling	Examinees use line and curve tools to sketch a given situation on a grid.	Bennett, Morley, & Quardt (2000); Bennett, Morley, Quardt, & Rock (2000)
Move figure or symbols in/into pictographs	Examinees manipulate elements of chart or graph to represent certain situations or adjust or complete image as necessary (e.g., extending bars in a bar chart, see Figure 2).	Educational Testing Service (1993); French & Godwin (1996); Martinez (1991)
Drag and connect, specifying relationships	Given presented objects, examinees identify the relationship(s) that exist between pairs of objects (see Figure 3).	Fitzgerald (2001); Luecht (2001)
Concept mapping	Examinees demonstrate knowledge of interrelationships between data points by graphically representing onscreen images and text using links and nodes.	Chung, O'Neil, & Herl (1999); Klein, O'Neil, & Baker (1998)
Sorting task	Given prototypes, examinees look for surface or deep structural similarities between presented items and prototypes and match items with prototype categories.	Bennett & Sebrechts (1997); Glaser (1991)
Ordering information (create-a-tree)	Examinees sequence events as required by item stem (e.g., largest to smallest, most to least probable cause of event, if–then; see Figure 4).	Educational Testing Service (1993); Fitzgerald (2001); Luecht (2001); Walker & Crandall (1999)
Inserting text	Examinees drag and drop text into passage as directed by item stem (e.g., where it makes sense, serves as example of observation).	Educational Testing Service (1993); Taylor, Jamieson, Eignor, & Kirsch (1998)
Passage editing	Examinees edit a short onscreen passage by moving the cursor to various points in a passage and selecting sentence rewrites from a list of alternatives on a drop-down menu.	Breland (1999); Davey, Godwin, & Mittelholtz (1997)

Item type	Description	References
Highlighting text	Examinees read a passage and select specific sentence(s) in the passage (e.g., main idea, particular piece of information).	Carey (2001); Taylor, Jamieson, Eignor, & Kirsch (1998); Walker & Crandall (1999)
Capturing or selecting frames/Shading	Given directions or parameters, examinees use mouse to select portion of picture, map, or graph.	Hambleton (1997); O'Neil & Folk (1996)
Mathematical expressions	Examinees generate and type in unique expression to represent mathematical relationship.	Bennett, Morley, & Quardt (2000); Bennett et al. (1997); Educational Testing Service (1993); Martinez & Bennett (1992)
Numerical equations	Examinees complete numerical sentences by entering numbers and mathematical symbols in text box.	Hambleton (1997)
Multiple numerical response	Examinees type in more than one numerical answer (e.g., complete tax form, insert numbers into a spreadsheet).	Hambleton (1997)
Multiple selection	Examinees are presented with a stimulus (visual, audio, text) and select answer(s) from list (answers may be used more than once in series of questions).	Ackerman, Evans, Park, Tamassia, & Turner (1999); Mills (2000)
Analyzing situations	Examinees are provided with visual/audio clips and short informational text and are asked to make diagnosis/decision. Response could be free-text entry or extended matching.	Ackerman, Evans, Park, Tamassia, & Turner (1999)
Generating examples	Examinees create examples given certain situations or constraints; there is more than one correct answer. Response is free-text entry.	Bennett, Morley, & Quardt (2000); Bennett et al. (1999); Enright, Rock, & Bennett (1998); Nhouyvanisvong, Katz, & Singley (1997)
Generating multiple solutions/Formulating hypotheses	Given situation, examinees generate plausible solutions or explanations. Response is free-text entry (see Figure 5).	Bennett & Rock (1995); Kaplan & Bennett (1994)
Essay/Short answer	May be restricted or extended length.	Burstein et al. (1998); Rizavi & Sireci (1999)
Problem-solving vignettes	Problem-solving situations (vignettes) are presented to examinees, who are graded on features of a product.	Bejar (1991); Fitzgerald (2001); Luecht (2001); Williamson, Bejar, & Hone (1999); Williamson, Hone, Miller, & Bejar (1998)
Sequential problem solving/Role play	Examinees provide a series of responses as dynamic situation unfolds. Scoring attends to process and product.	Clauser, Harik, & Clyman (2000); Clauser et al. (1997)

Our discussion of novel item types begins with those items requiring use of the mouse for different onscreen actions as methods for data collection. Some of these item types bear greater resemblance to traditional selected response item types and are easier to score mechanically, whereas others integrate technology in more inventive ways. After introducing these item types, we turn to those item types involving text-based responses. Last, we focus on items with more complex examinee responses that expand the concept of what responses to test items look like in fundamental ways and pose more difficult challenges for automated scoring.

Item types requiring use of a mouse.   Many of the emerging computer-based item types take advantage of the way in which people interact with a computer, specifically via a keyboard and mouse. The mouse and onscreen cursor provide a flexible mechanism by which items can be manipulated. Using a mouse, pull-down menus, and arrow keys, examinees can highlight text, drag-and-drop text and other stimuli, create drawings or graphics, or point to critical features of an item. An example of a drag-and-drop item (also called a *select-and-place* item) is presented in Figure 1. This item type is used on a number of the Microsoft certifi-

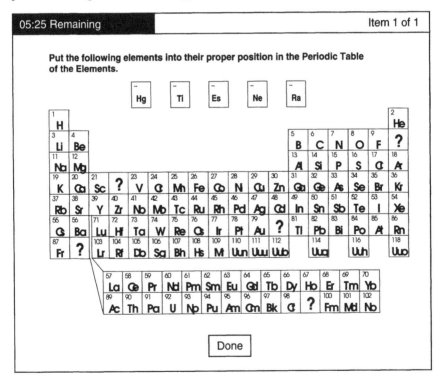

FIGURE 1   Example of drag-and-drop item type.

cation examinations (Fitzgerald, 2001; Microsoft Corporation, 1998). These items can be scored right/wrong or using partial credit.

The *graphical modeling* item type also uses the drag-and-drop capability of a computer. This item type requires examinees to sketch out situations graphically using onscreen line, curve tools, or both (Bennett, Morley, & Quardt, 2000; Bennett, Morley, Quardt, & Rock, 2000). A similar item type using drag-and-drop technology is the *move figures or symbols into pictographs* item type, which is presented in Figure 2. This item type requires examinees to drag a shape and position it on a grid given certain parameters or constraints in the item stem (French & Godwin, 1996; Martinez, 1991).

A variation of the drag-and-drop item is the *drag-and-connect* item type. This item type presents examinees with several movable objects that can be arranged in several different target locations onscreen. For example, when all the objects are correctly assembled (items are sequenced or organized accurately), a network would correctly work or a flowchart would appropriately illustrate a network protocol. An extension of this item type is the *specifying relationships* item type in which examinees move objects around onscreen and link them in a flowchart by way of clicking relationships such as "one to one," "many to one," or "one to zero" (Fitzgerald, 2001; Luecht, 2001). An example of this item type is presented in Figure 3. Another item type that can be used to assess the understanding of relation-

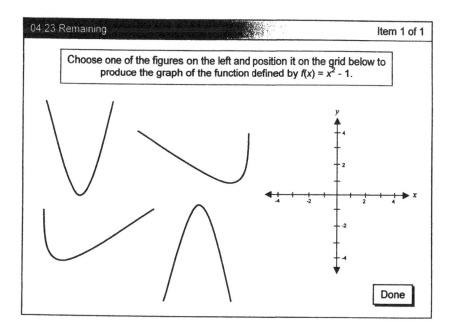

FIGURE 2   Example of moving figures or symbols in/into a pictograph item type.

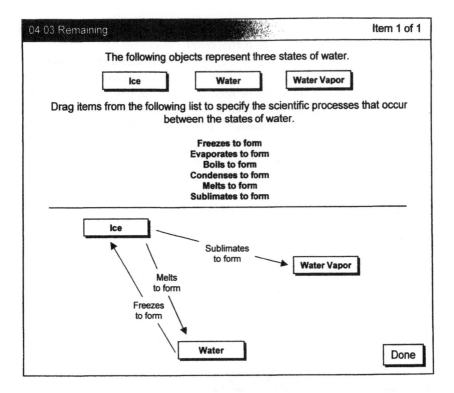

FIGURE 3   Example of specifying relationships item type.

ships is the *concept map* item type. Having an examinee create onscreen concept maps can allow for relationships between items or pieces of information to be illustrated (Chung, O'Neil, & Herl, 1999; Herl, O'Neil, Chung, & Schacter, 1999; Klein, O'Neil, & Baker, 1998).

Items that delve into assessing ordering and sorting information are increasingly using drag-and-drop action. Bennett's and Sebrechts' (1997) *sorting task* item type (also studied by Glaser, 1991) gives examinees the chance to communicate knowledge about underlying relationships between items by dragging and dropping focal items onto the target prototype to which it best aligns according to some surface or deep structural feature.

The *ordering information* item type, also referred to in the literature as a *create-a-tree* item, requires examinees to use the mouse to exhibit understanding of the material tested. The stem of this item type specifies the way in which the examinee should arrange elements in a process. The examinee clicks on a focal object and then places it into a target location by dragging and dropping or by clicking on onscreen radio buttons to move the item as needed (Fitzgerald, 2001;

Luecht, 2001; Walker & Crandall, 1999). Some sequences in which these focal items might be arranged include largest to smallest, most-to-least probable cause of an event, or following an if–then framework. Figure 4 presents an example of an ordering information/create-a-tree item type.

Some computer-based item types are used to assess skills specifically relating to verbal communication and comprehension skills. One, the *inserting text* item type, presents examinees with a sentence that must be dragged and dropped into the appropriate place in a passage (Carey, 2001; Jamieson, Taylor, Kirsch, & Eignor, 1998). A similar item type is the *passage editing* item; the examinees move the cursor to various onscreen "hot spots" where a drop-down menu appears with a list of potential sentence or phrase rewrites, and the examinee must select the best alternative from the list (Breland, 1999; Davey, Godwin, & Mittelholtz, 1997). The alternatives could range from radical changes to no change at all, with the different options being scored correct/incorrect or using a graded scale.

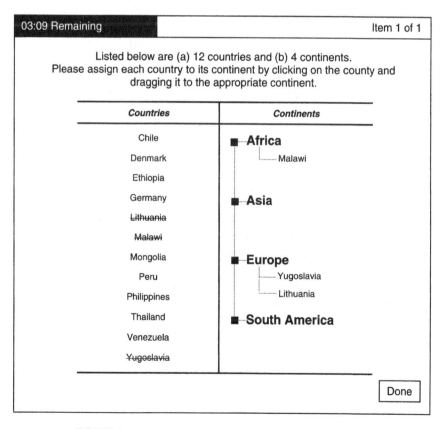

FIGURE 4   Example of ordering information/create-a-tree item type.

Another objectively scorable item type that uses mouse manipulation is the *highlighting information* item type where the examinee uses the cursor to select a target phrase or sentence within a passage. Examples of this item type include identifying the main idea of a paragraph or antecedents of pronouns (Carey, 2001; Taylor, Jamieson, Eignor, & Kirsch, 1998; Walker & Crandall, 1999). A similar item type is the *capturing/selecting frames* item type (sometimes also referred to as *shading*) that directs the examinee to click on portions of a graphic as needed (Hambleton, 1997; O'Neil & Folk, 1996).

The item types described thus far could be described as "click-on item types," as clicking on one or more objects is required. For all of these item types examinees must select or highlight information as directed by the item stem by moving the mouse, which correspondingly moves an onscreen cursor. Many of these item types might be considered by some as little more than extended multiple-choice items, but generally with such items the objects that could be selected are so numerous they require skills above and beyond the test-taking skills helpful for success on traditional selected-response items. The *multiple selection* item type is a good example of an item with this property, in that the examinee is expected to select text or onscreen items using the mouse given instructions such as "choose all that apply" or "select three" (Ackerman, Evans, Park, Tamassia, & Turner, 1999; Mills, 2000). Obviously, such items reduce the chance of answering the item correctly by guessing, relative to a traditional multiple-choice item.

Innovations in items with text-based responses.   Moving from the mouse to the keyboard as the mechanism for examinees to enter responses, a number of both novel and more familiar item types become increasingly useful in large-scale performance assessment. Although having an examinee write a short answer or an essay in a text box is not particularly novel, collecting such answers via computer can be effective for data management purposes and is increasingly likely to be the preferred method of evaluating writing skills (to the extent that typing is accepted as a skill directed relevant to the construct(s) of interest). Similarly, in the *mathematical expressions*, *numerical equations*, and *multiple numerical response* item types, the examinee can type answers into free-response text boxes (Bennett, Morley, & Quardt, 2000; Bennett, Steffen, Singley, Morley, & Jacquemin, 1997). Although these item types may not be especially innovative in and of themselves, the responses can be surprisingly complex to complete, manage, and score because there are multiple ways in which any mathematical or text-based response could be expressed.

One novel item type in which examinees respond by means of a text box is the *generating examples* item type. Problems and constraints are presented to the examinee, whose task it is to pose one or several solutions that are feasible under such parameters (Bennett, Morley, & Quardt, 2000; Bennett et al., 1999; Enright, Rock, & Bennett, 1998; Nhouyvanisvong, Katz, & Singley, 1997). In some applications of this item type, the responses are numerical in answer. In fact, it was originally designed in part to broaden the measurement of the construct "quantitative reasoning" on the Graduate Record Examination, or GRE. Generating examples, as an item type, is a variant of the *generating solutions/formulating hypotheses* item type (Bennett & Rock, 1995; Kaplan & Bennett, 1994), an example of which is presented in Figure 5. In the formulating hypotheses item type, an examinee is first presented with a situation of some kind. The task then is to generate as many possible explanations or causal reasonings for the situation as possible.

Complex constructed-response items for CBT.   Some of the most intriguing advances in CBT are the *problem solving vignettes* used on professional licensure exams. Typically, the vignettes presented to licensure candidates reflect real-world problems, and the computer simulates real-world responses. An example of this increased fidelity in measurement is the problem solving vignette item type found on the Architectural Registration Examination (ARE). On the ARE, examinees are asked to complete several design tasks (such as design a building or lay out a parking lot) using a variety of onscreen drawing tools (Bejar, 1991; William-

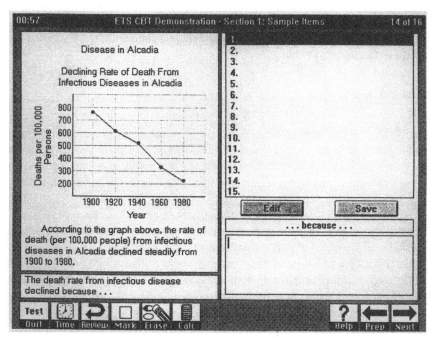

FIGURE 5   Example of formulating hypotheses/generating solutions item type. Source: The formulating-hypotheses item type. (n.d.). Retrieved February 26, 2001, from http://www.ets.org/research/rsc/alcadia.html Copyright © Educational Testing Service. Used with permission.

son, Bejar, & Hone, 1999; Williamson, Hone, Miller, & Bejar, 1998). By and large, these items *seem* highly authentic to examinees and give test users data about examinee ability in relation to actual, standardized architectural design tasks. In this case, the generalizability of test item to job performance as described by Kane (1992) is high.

Closely related to such problem-solving vignettes are *dynamic problem solving tasks*, sometimes referred to as role-play exercises. In measurement, we typically think of adaptive testing as dynamic between items, but advances in computer hardware and software now allow some testing programs to create tests that are adaptive within an item, where an item may be defined as an extended role-playing task. The computerized case-based simulations used by the National Board of Medical Examiners incorporate the idea of the simulated patient whose symptoms and vital statistics change over time in response to the actions (or nonactions) taken by the candidate (Clauser, Harik, & Clyman, 2000; Clauser, Margolis, Clyman, & Ross, 1997). As the examinee manages a case, new symptoms may emerge, the clock is ticking, and the prospective doctor's actions have the potential to harm as well as help the simulated patient. As the case progresses, the examinee may have to deal with unintended medical side effects as well as the patient's original medical condition. Each examinee is scored on the sequence of response actions they enter into the computer, such as requesting tests on the patient, writing treatment orders, and their diagnostic acuity. Similar dynamic simulation tasks are used for aviation selection and training.

Media in Item Stems

A further emerging dimension of novel item types relates to what Parshall, Davey, and Pashley (2000) referred to as *media inclusion*: the use of graphics, video, and audio within an item or set of items. Multimedia can be used at various points in the item stem for a variety of purposes: to better illustrate a particular situation, to allow examinees to visualize a problem, or to better assess a specified construct (e.g., music-listening aptitude).

Audio prompts in large-scale, noncomputerized testing have been largely confined to music and language tests, with partial success in those areas. However, Parshall and Balizet (2001) defined a framework for considering four uses of an audio component in CBTs, including speech audio for listening tests, nonspeech audio (e.g., music) for listening tests, speech audio for alternative assessment (such as accommodating tests for limited-English proficient, reading disabled, or visually disabled examinees), and speech and nonspeech audio incorporated into the user interface. From a measurement perspective, as Vispoel (1999) noted, when tests of music listening or aptitude are administered to a group in a non-CBT format, compromises in administrative efficiency and measurement accuracy often leave examinee scores on such tests with questionable reliability. The difference in a computer-based setting is that the test can be administered individually and this format of test administration permits examinees to proceed at their own pace (Parshall & Balizet, 2001). An example of the successful use of audio prompts in large-scale computer-based assessment is Educational Testing Service's (ETS's) Test of English as a Foreign Language, which incorporates such features.

Graphics, on the other hand, have generally enjoyed more extensive use in computerized assessment. For example, the presentation of digitized pictures has been used successfully by Ackerman, Evans, Park, Tamassia, and Turner (1999) in a test of dermatological skin disorders. Examinees can use a zoom feature to get a better look at the picture before selecting the correct diagnosis from a list of 110 alphabetized disorders. Although this item type would be strictly classified as a selected-response item, rather than constructed-response, the emulation of the diagnostic processes of professional dermatologists allows examinees to demonstrate a higher order grasp of the information and reduces the likelihood of guessing. On other tests, onscreen images can be rotated, resized, selected, clicked on, and dragged to form a meaningful image, depending on the item type (Klein, O'Neil, & Baker, 1998). Some of the items described in Table 1, including graphical modeling, concept mapping, and moving a figure into a graph, are examples of tasks where the graphical manipulations compose the constructed responses.

Furthermore, most desktop computers now have video capabilities that make the inclusion of video prompts in performance assessment highly feasible. Interactive video assessment has been used operationally with the Workplace Situations test at IBM (Desmarais et al., 1992), the Allstate Multimedia In-Basket (Ashworth & Joyce, 1994), and the Conflict Resolution Skills Assessment (Drasgow, Olson-Buchanan, & Moberg, 1999). In the Conflict Resolutions Skills Assessment, for example, an examinee views a conflict scene of approximately 2 minutes' duration, which stops at a critical point and asks the examinee to select one of four response options. Based on this selection, action branches out and continues until a second critical point is reached, and so forth.

Although selected response may be easier to implement due to a test developer's desire to avoid the infinite number of possible solutions when constructed responses are used, it is possible to envision a day in the near future when advanced computing technology such as virtual reality might be used to more dynamically model interactive situations and complex software applications are developed to score them successfully.

Use of Reference Materials

One additional new facet of how examinees complete items is the extent to which examinees may use reference materials as they go through the test. On some assessments, examinees can use calculators or other reference materials. Indeed, calculators may be used on the SAT I (College Board, 2000b) and the ACT Mathematics test (American College Testing Program, 2000) and are required on two of the mathematics sections of the SAT II (College Board, 2000a). In terms of a credentialing/licensure test, one section of the mathematics assessment of the Praxis teacher certification test specifically prohibits calculators, one section allows them, and other sections require them (ETS, 2000). The ARE also requires examinees to supply their own calculators.

Additional examples of auxiliary information examinees may access are found on the credentialing examinations administered for Novell software certification and on the ARE. One of Novell's certification exams measures candidates' ability to quickly navigate two reference CDs to locate information necessary to complete a task (D. Foster, personal communication, April 11, 2000). One CD contains technical product information, and the other contains a technical library detailing information about cables, hard drives, monitors, and CPUs. The tasks tap the candidates' ability to "research" these CDs to locate the content necessary to solve a problem. The ARE also allows candidates to access resource material via the computer. Candidates can retrieve certain subject specific information about building code requirements, program constraints, and vignette specifications on demand as they design structures in accordance with the presented task directions (National Council of Architectural Registration Boards, 2000).

Novell certification exams have an additional interactive feature: Candidates who take a non-English version of an exam can access the English-language version of each item. If they so desire, candidates can click on a button to switch back and forth between the language in which they are taking the test and English (Foster, Olsen, Ford, & Sireci, 1997).

INNOVATIONS IN SCORING COMPLEX
CONSTRUCTED-RESPONSES

Computerized-adaptive testing (CAT) is increasingly attractive to test developers as a way to increase the amount of information examinee responses provide about ability. However, as Parshall, Davey, and Pashley (2000) point out, an adaptive test works best if the computer can score examinee responses to the test items automatically and instantaneously. This has not historically been a problem when the items being used are selected-response, as the computer can easily compare the sequence of response from each examinee to the programmed answer key. The traditional multiple-choice item, scored with a dichotomous item response model, is the item type principally used in CAT, but some variations on the multiple-choice item, such as multiple numerical response, graphical modeling, drag-and-drop, multiple selection, and ordering information might also be scored fairly easily using a polytomous item response model.

A problem in incorporating many of the innovative performance tasks in Table 1 into a CAT format or into a linear CBT, however, is that each examinee provides a unique response for each item. Thus, the structure and nature of those answers may vary widely across examinees, and scoring decisions cannot typically be made immediately using mechanical application of limited, explicit criteria (Bennett, Sebrechts, & Rock, 1991). Legitimate logistical difficulties in automatically scoring these responses might at first seem to preclude the manufacture of CAT performance assessments, although a CBT format might be feasible (as scoring occurs at a later date). However, current developments in psychology, computer science, communication disorders, and artificial intelligence reveal several promising directions for the future of computerized performance assessment.

Clearly, a consideration in terms of automated scoring is the level of constraint desired in the constructed response. Among the various constructed-response item types, it is possible to constrain any individual item in such a way that there are several or infinite possible answers, just as an item can be written to ensure that there is only one correct response. Take a graphical modeling problem, for example, where the task is to model the developments of an interest-bearing account. This could be highly specific, such that given a base amount of money, an interest rate, and a length of time, an examinee would use the mouse to graphically represent an outcome. Alternatively, given certain information the examinee could be asked to extrapolate future outcomes from current data, and in this case (depending on how an examinee synthesized the available information) there might be more than one appropriate way to respond graphically.

Currently, much of the work in terms of automated scoring has focused on developing techniques for scoring essays, computer programs, simulated patient interactions, and architectural designs online. The most prominent computer-based scoring methods, described in the following sections, are summarized in Table 2. These scoring methods fall into three general categories: essay scoring, expert systems analysis, and mental modeling.

Automated Scoring of Essays

Essays are perhaps the most common form of constructed responses used in large-scale assessment, although their use is limited because many testing programs need two and sometimes three humans to read and evaluate essays according to preestablished scoring rubrics. Other constructed-response text-based item types typically found on paper-and-pencil tests, such as the accounting problems on the Uniform Certified Public Accountants Examination, are scored in a similarly labor-intensive fashion. Given the expense of extensively training readers, who are required to establish score validity, computerized alternatives to human readers are highly attractive. Research on automated scoring programs and methods for the most part have demonstrated the comparability of essay scoring across

TABLE 2
Summary of Automated Scoring Programs/Methods

Scoring Method	Description	Citation(s)
Essays/Free-text answers		
Project essay grade	Uses a regression model where the independent variables are surface features of the text (document length, word length, and punctuation) and the dependent variable is the essay score.	Page (1994)
E-rater	Evaluates numerous structural and linguistic features specified in a holistic scoring guide using natural language process techniques.	Burstein & Chodorow (in press); Burstein et al. (1998)
Latent semantic analysis	A theory and method for extracting and representing the contextual usage of words by statistical computations applied to a large corpus of text.	Foltz, Kintsch, & Landauer (1998); Landauer, Foltz, & Laham (1998); Landauer et al. (1997)
Text categorization	Evaluates text using automated learning techniques to categorize text documents, where linguistic expressions and contexts extracted from the texts are used to classify texts.	Larkey (1998)
Constructed free response scoring tool	Scores short verbal answers, where examinees key in responses that are pattern-matched to programmed correct responses.	Martinez & Bennett (1992)
Expert systems	Examinee's completed response is compared to a problem-specific knowledge base encoded within the computer's memory banks. The knowledge base is constructed from human content-expert responses that have been coded in a machine-usable form.	Bennett & Sebrechts (1996); Braun et al. (1990); Martinez & Bennett (1992); Sebrechts, Bennett, & Rock (1991)
Mental modeling	Elements of the final product can be evaluated against the universe of all possible variations using a process that mimics the scoring processing of committees and requires an analysis of the way experts evaluate solutions. Scores can be compared to the results obtained from human raters to assess agreement.	Bejar (1991); Clauser (2000); Clauser, Harik, & Clyman (2000); Clauser et al. (1997); Martinez & Bennett (1992); Williamson, Bejar, & Hone (1999); Williamson, et al. (1998)

human and computer graders (Burstein, Kukich, Wolff, Lu, & Chodorow, 1998; Rizavi & Sireci, 1999; Yang, Buckendahl, Juszkiewicz, & Bhola, 2002). Currently, several computerized essay scoring options and methods are available, including project essay grade (PEG), e-rater, latent semantic analysis, text categorization, and the constructed-response scoring tool.

Project essay grade.   PEG, developed by Ellis Page in the mid-1960s, was the first automated essay grading system; the current version evolved from his earlier work (Page, 1994; Page & Petersen, 1995). Like most computerized essay scoring programs, the specifics of how PEG works are proprietary. However, descriptions of the program suggest that it uses multiple regression to determine the optimal combination of the surface features of an essay (e.g., average word length, essay word length, number of uncommon words, number of commas) as well as complex structure of the essay (e.g., soundness of sentence structure) to best predict the score that would be assigned by a human grader (Page, 1994, Page & Petersen, 1995). By assigning weights to these surface and intrinsic features, the computer attempts to mimic human scoring. Although it is unclear whether PEG is currently being used in large-scale assessment, it is clear that it set the stage for other developments in the computerized scoring of essays.

E-rater.   E-rater (Burstein et al., 1998; Burstein & Chodorow, in press) is the essay scoring system developed by ETS for the essay portion of the Graduate Management Admissions Test (GMAT). It is designed to evaluate numerous structural and linguistic features specified in a holistic scoring guide. On the GMAT, each examinee responds to two essay questions, which are scored by both a trained human grader and an electronic reader. Currently, e-rater serves as the second reader. If human and e-rater scores on a particular essay differ by more than one point, the essay is sent to a second human expert, and finally, if consensus is still not reached, to a final human referee. Thus, the GMAT scoring system provides an example of how the computer can be used to increase the efficiency of essay scoring while maintaining the validity of the final scores assigned to an essay.

Latent semantic analysis.   Latent semantic analysis (LSA) is a theory and method for extracting and representing the contextual usage of words by statistical computations applied to a large corpus of text (Foltz, Kintsch, & Landauer, 1998; Landauer, Foltz, & Laham, 1998; Rehder et al., 1998). The underlying idea is that the aggregate of all the word contexts in which a given word does and does not appear provides a set of mutual constraints that largely determines the similarity of meaning of words and sets of words to each other. A possible analogy for LSA could be the way multidimensional scaling allows relationships between variables to be plotted in n dimensions. In LSA, words can be mapped into semantic space and distances between words are derived from shadings of meaning, which are obtained through context. LSA's algorithm has a learning component that "reads" through a text and develops an understanding of the sentence or passage by evolving a meaning for each word in relation to all the other words in the sentence or passage. The LSA system can be "trained" to work in different content areas by having it electronically read texts relevant to the domain of interest. One possible caveat to the use of LSA: At this time, the algorithm does not derive sentence meaning from word order, which is a possible place for exploitation, but ongoing research addresses this point (Landauer, Laham, Rehder, & Schreiner, 1997).

Text categorization.   Text categorization is a method for evaluating text that uses automated learning techniques to categorize documents, where linguistic expressions and contexts extracted from the texts are used to classify them (Larkey, 1998). This type of analysis is informed by work in areas of machine learning, Bayesian networks, information retrieval, natural language processing, case-based reasoning, language modeling, and speech recognition. A number of text categorization algorithms have been developed, incorporating different schema for classifying text. The sorting of verbal content may be related to topic, to specified levels of quality, or perhaps by keywords. It is interesting that the evaluation of essays is only one of the many situations in which text categorization techniques have been applied. These algorithms are also used in sorting documents in databases in an information retrieval context such as in the code that powers Internet search engines. One organization with ongoing research into text categorization is the Edinburgh Language Technology Group (http://www.ltg.ed.ac.uk/papers/class.html). On this Web site, this group details much of their work on multiple applications of text categorization methodology.

The Constructed Free Response Scoring Tool.   The Constructed Free Response Scoring Tool (FRST) is an automated approach to scoring examinee's constructed responses online (Martinez & Bennett, 1992). FRST is an algorithm developed to score short verbal answers, where examinees key in responses that are pattern-matched to programmed correct responses (Martinez & Bennett, 1992). FRST has a 100% congruence rate with human raters when examinee responses range in length between 5 and 7 words, and an 88% congruence rate for responses between 12 and 15 words. In this case, *congruence rate* is defined as the rate at which scores assigned to examinee responses by the computer and the human rater exactly match.

Expert Systems Analysis

Expert systems analysis provides another example of the use of computers to score complex examinee responses. Expert systems are computer programs designed to emulate the scoring behaviors of human content specialists. Expert scoring has been studied in a number of contexts, including computer programming and mathematics problems. For example, PROUST and MicroPROUST are two expert systems developed to automatically score computer programs that examinees write using the Pascal language (Braun, Bennett, Frye, & Soloway, 1990; Martinez & Bennett, 1992). Each system has knowledge to reason about programming problems within intention-based analysis framework. Based on how humans reason out computer programs, the expert systems analysis formulates deep-structure, goal, and plan representation in the process of trying to identify nonsyntactical errors.

In terms of constructed-response quantitative items, the expert scoring system known as GIDE produces a series of comments about errors present in examinees' solutions and then incorporates that information into computation of partial-credit scores (Bennett & Sebrechts, 1996; Martinez & Bennett, 1992; Sebrechts, Bennett, & Rock, 1991). The expert systems program consults a problem-specific knowledge base constructed from human content-expert responses that are coded in a machine-usable form. The examinee responses are broken down into component parts, and each piece is evaluated against multiple programmed alternatives. Here, analysis has shown that reasonable machine-rater congruence can be obtained (e.g., a .86 correlation between the scores assigned to essays by a machine and by a human rater; Martinez & Bennett, 1992). Interestingly, research into GIDE, PROUST, and MicroPROUST expert systems scoring mechanisms suggests that although each is highly accurate at classifying examinee responses as correct or incorrect, they are less able to provide specific diagnostic information about examinee errors.

Mental Modeling

An additional approach to computerized scoring of complex performance tasks is mental modeling, which is currently used to score portions of the ARE. The performance tasks on the ARE are often cited as highly interactive and innovative examples of the possibilities that exist for automated scoring in computer-based testing. Examinees are presented with architectural design tasks given various constraints and, in effect, create blueprints for buildings during the testing session. Each problem is graded on four attributes (grammatical, code compliance, diagrammatic compliance, and design logic and efficiency) using features extraction analysis where elements of the final product can be evaluated against the universe of all possible variations (Bejar, 1991; Martinez & Bennett, 1992). Various elements extracted from an examinee's constructed response are compared to the universe of possible variations where the components of possible responses are evaluated using a procedure that mimics the scoring processing of committees and requires an analysis of the way experienced experts evaluate solutions (Williamson, Bejar, & Hone, 1999). This "mental modeling" approach to scoring, done by computers, can be compared to the results obtained from human raters to assess the extent to which these methodologies agree on results.

In addition to being used on the ARE, the National Board of Medical Examiners has incorporated the mental model algorithm into its patient care simulations (Clauser, Harik, & Clyman, 2000; Clauser et al., 1997). Each action that examinees key in is varyingly associated as benefitting the simulated patient or as an inappropriate action carrying some level of risk. Features extraction analysis and mental modeling may be applicable as a medium for the automated scoring of essays as well, where the features could be specified as components of an essay, such as sentences.

The various algorithms for automatically scoring constructed responses represent an especially exciting direction for computerized assessment practices. Using computers in this regard will help to improve the extent to which uniformity and precision in scoring rules can be implemented (Clauser et al., 2000). As a result, test users and examinees alike may develop greater confidence in the inferences about domain proficiency made on the basis of test scores. Likewise, as Bennett (1998) mentioned, delivery efficiency will improve. In consequence, performance tasks that can be automatically evaluated will become more logistically and practically feasible for use in high-stakes credentialing.

DIRECTIONS FOR FUTURE RESEARCH

The incorporation of different response actions, task formats, multimedia prompts, and reference materials into test items has the potential to substantially increase the types of skills, abilities, and processes that can be measured. Likewise, the implementation of automated scoring methods can greatly facilitate the processing of examinee responses. The potential benefits of incorporating these innovations and tasks to testing are great, but such benefits cannot fully materialize without further research on a number of psychometric and operational concerns (particularly with regard to many of the emerging item types, as found by Zenisky & Sireci, 2001). Technology-related dimensions of test format, administration, and scoring cannot be accepted without due psychometric scrutiny.

In terms of integrating innovations in task presentation into more large-scale assessments, there are a several critical directions for research. The intricacy of the task and how it relates to the skill(s) being assessed in a given testing context is an issue of central importance that must be rigorously evaluated (Crocker, 1997). Examinees should not be overwhelmed with innovative item types and item features that are extraneous to the task. To this end, the relative simplicity or complexity of the user interface should remain a fundamental concern for test developers, especially in light of the potential for gadgetry to eclipse real technological benefits. Oftentimes, extended tutorials may be necessary to sufficiently familiarize examinees with novel testing tasks, and thus use of these types may require substantial testing time and development resource commitments from test developers. Further research specific to different types and task presentation variables can help determine the kinds of preparation and tutorials necessary for this purpose.

Practical validity concerns in CBT include the adequacy of construct representation (Huff & Sireci, 2001; Kane, Crooks, & Cohen, 1999; Messick, 1995) and task generalizability (Brennan & Johnson, 1995; Linn & Burton, 1994; Shavelson, Baxter, & Pine, 1991). Issues of task specificity such as the relative number of tasks and the extent to which examinee performance can be generalized from the selected tasks (Guion, 1995) are additional concerns. Equally important are studies to determine potential sources of construct-irrelevant variance associated with such item types (Huff & Sireci, 2001). Furthermore, work to evaluate adverse impact for different subgroups of examinee populations has by and large not been completed for most emerging item types. This problem needs to be addressed in future research.

Automated scoring must be evaluated with respect to potential losses in score validity, perhaps in the direction of multitrait–multimethod analyses (Clauser, 2000; Yang et al., 2002). The emerging area of multidimensional item response theory (IRT) models may provide some interesting ways for scoring complex constructed responses (see Ackerman, 1994, and van der Linden & Hambleton, 1997, for further information on multidimensional IRT). Preliminary research suggests that compromises in reliability and information per minute of testing time may occur when complex, computerized constructed-response item types are used (Jodoin, 2001), so further research in the areas of reliability and test and item information should be accelerated.

CONCLUSIONS

Technological advances in CBT represent positive future directions for the evaluation of complex performances within large-scale testing programs, especially given the escalating use of technology in many aspects of everyday life. Examinees support the opportunity to demonstrate what they know when tasks on a test more faithfully relate to the skills necessary for a particular domain, and these methods may provide test users with ways to acquire information about an examinee's proficiency on a given knowledge or skill area more directly (Kane, 1992). As psychometric research related to computerized performance assessment is completed, the application of empirical results with regard to fusions of technology and measurement will continue to impact positively on assessment practices.

The overview of emerging technological innovations in computer-based assessment presented in this article provides a comprehensive (although not exhaustive) description of numerous recent developments in computer-based assessment.

Many of these innovations have both strengths and weaknesses from practical and psychometric perspectives, and thus enthusiasm for these emerging measurement methods must be tempered by scientific wariness about their technical characteristics. Still, although it is difficult to predict the future, many of these CBT innovations are likely to dramatically change the testing experience for many examinees who sit for assessments in a wide variety of testing contexts, including certification and licensure, admissions, and achievement testing.

ACKNOWLEDGMENTS

Laboratory of Psychometric and Evaluative Research Report No. 383, School of Education, University of Massachusetts, Amherst. This research was funded in part by the American Institute of Certified Public Accountants (AICPA). We are grateful for this support. The opinions expressed in this article are ours and do not represent official positions of the AICPA.

REFERENCES

Ackerman, T. A. (1994). Using multidimensional item response theory to understand what items and tests are measuring. *Applied Measurement in Education, 7,* 255–278.

Ackerman, T. A., Evans, J., Park, K., Tamassia, C., & Turner, R. (1999). Computer assessment using visual stimuli: A test of dermatological skin disorders. In F. Drasgow and J. B. Olson-Buchanan (Eds.), *Innovations in computerized assessment* (pp. 137–150). Mahwah, NJ: Lawrence Erlbaum Associates, Inc.

American College Testing Program. (2000). *Calculators and the ACT math test.* Retrieved March 20, 2000, from http://www.act.org/aap/taking/calculator.html

Ashworth, S. D., & Joyce, T. M. (1994, April). *Developing scoring protocols for a computerized multimedia in-basket exercise.* Paper presented at the Ninth Annual Conference of the Society for Industrial and Organizational Psychology, Nashville, TN.

Bejar, I. (1991). A methodology for scoring open-ended architectural design problems. *Journal of Applied Psychology, 76,* 522–532.

Bennett, R. E. (1998). *Reinventing assessment: Speculations on the future of large-scale educational testing.* Princeton, NJ: Educational Testing Service.

Bennett, R. E., Morley, M., & Quardt, D. (2000). Three response types for broadening the conception of mathematical problem solving in computerized-adaptive tests. *Applied Psychological Measurement, 24,* 294–309.

Bennett, R. E., Morley, M., Quardt, D., & Rock, D. A. (2000). Graphical modeling: A new response type for measuring the qualitative component of mathematical reasoning. *Applied Measurement in Education, 13,* 303–322.

Bennett, R. E., Morley, M., Quardt, D., Rock, D. A., Singley, M. K., Katz, I. R., & Nhouyvanisvong, A. (1999). Psychometric and cognitive functioning of an under-determined computer-based response type for quantitative reasoning. *Journal of Educational Measurement, 36,* 233–252.

Bennett, R. E., & Rock, D. A. (1995). Generalizability, validity, and examinee perceptions of a computer-delivered formulating-hypotheses test. *Journal of Educational Measurement, 32,* 19–36.

Bennett, R. E., & Sebrechts, M. M. (1996). The accuracy of expert-system diagnoses of mathematical problem solutions. *Applied Measurement in Education, 9,* 133–150.

Bennett, R. E., & Sebrechts, M. M. (1997). A computer-based task for measuring the representational component of quantitative proficiency. *Journal of Educational Measurement, 34,* 64–78.

Bennett, R. E., Sebrechts, M. M., & Rock, D. A. (1991). Expert system scores for complex constructed-response quantitative items: A study of convergent validity. *Applied Psychological Measurement, 15,* 227–239.

Bennett, R. E., Steffen, M., Singley, M. K., Morley, M., & Jacquemin, D. (1997). Evaluating an automatically scorable, open-ended response type for measuring mathematical reasoning in computer-adaptive tests. *Journal of Educational Measurement, 34,* 162–176.

Braun, H. I., Bennett, R. E., Frye, D., & Soloway, E. (1990). Scoring constructed responses using expert systems. *Journal of Educational Measurement, 27,* 93–108.

Breland, H. M. (1999). *Exploration of an automated editing task as a GRE writing measure* (RR–99–9). Princeton, NJ: Educational Testing Service.

Brennan, R. L., & Johnson, E. G. (1995). Generalizability of performance assessments. *Educational Measurement: Issues and Practice, 14*(4), 25–27.

Burstein, J., & Chodorow, M. (2002). Directions in automated essay scoring analysis. In R. Kaplan (Ed.), *Oxford handbook of applied linguistics* (pp. 487–497). Oxford, England: Oxford University Press.

Burstein, J., Kukich, K., Wolff, S., Lu, C., & Chodorow, M. (1998, April). *Computer analysis of essays.* Paper presented at the NCME Symposium on Automated Scoring, San Diego, CA.

Carey, P. (2001, April). *Overview of current computer-based TOEFL.* Paper presented at the annual meeting of the National Council on Measurement in Education, Seattle, WA.

Chung, G. K. W. K., O'Neil, H. F., Jr., & Herl, H. E. (1999). The use of computer-based collaborative knowledge mapping to measure team processes and outcomes. *Computers in Human Behavior, 15,* 463–494.

Clauser, B. E. (2000). Recurrent issues and recent advances in scoring performance assessments. *Applied Psychological Measurement, 24,* 310–324.

Clauser, B. E., Harik, P., & Clyman, S. G. (2000). The generalizability of scores for a performance assessment scored with a computer-automated scoring system. *Journal of Educational Measurement, 37,* 245–261.

Clauser, B. E., Margolis, M. J., Clyman, S. G., & Ross, L. P. (1997). Development of automated scoring algorithms for complex performance assessments: A comparison of two approaches. *Journal of Educational Measurement, 34,* 141–161.

College Board. (2000a). *AP Calculus for the new century.* Retrieved March 20, 2000, from http://www.collegeboard.org/index_this/ap/calculus/new_century/evolution.html

College Board. (2000b). *Calculators.* Retrieved March 20, 2000, from http://www.collegeboard.org/index_this/sat/center/html/counselors/prep009.html

Crocker, L. (1997). Assessing content representativeness of performance assessment exercises. *Applied Measurement in Education, 10,* 83–95.

Davey, T., Godwin, J., & Mittelholtz, D. (1997). Developing and scoring an innovative computerized writing assessment. *Journal of Educational Measurement, 34,* 21–42.

Desmarais, L. B., Dyer, P. J., Midkiff, K. R., Barbera, K. M., Curtis, J. R., Esrig, F. H., & Masi, D. L. (1992, May). *Scientific uncertainties in the development of a multimedia test: Trade-offs and decisions.* Paper presented at the Seventh Annual Conference of the Society for Industrial and Organizational Psychology, Montreal, Quebec, Canada.

Drasgow, F., Olson-Buchanan, J. B., & Moberg, P. J. (1999). Development of an interactive video assessment: Trials and tribulations. In F. Drasgow & J. B. Olson-Buchanan (Eds.), *Innovations in computerized assessment* (pp. 197–219). Mahwah, NJ: Lawrence Erlbaum Associates, Inc.

Educational Testing Service. (1993). *Tests at a glance: Praxis I: Academic Skills Assessment.* Princeton, NJ: Author.

Educational Testing Service. (2000). *The Praxis Series: Professional Assessments for Beginning Teachers: Tests and test dates.* Retrieved March 20, 2000, from http://www.teachingandlearning.org/licensure/ praxis/prxtest.html

Enright, M. K., Rock, D. A., & Bennett, R. E. (1998). Improving measurement for graduate admissions. *Journal of Educational Measurement, 35,* 250–267.

Fitzgerald, C. (2001, April). *Rewards and challenges of implementing an innovative CBT certification exam program.* Paper presented at the annual meeting of the National Council on Measurement in Education, Seattle, WA.

Foltz, P. W., Kintsch, W., & Landauer, T. K. (1998). The measurement of textual coherence with latent semantic analysis. *Discourse Processes, 25,* 285–307.

Foster, D., Olsen, J. B., Ford, J., & Sireci, S. G. (1997, March). *Administering computerized certification exams in multiple languages: Lessons learned from the international marketplace.* Paper presented at the meeting of the American Educational Research Association, Chicago.

French, A., & Godwin, J. (1996). *Using multimedia technology to create innovative items.* Paper presented at the annual meeting of the American Educational Research Association, New York.

Glaser, R. (1991). Expertise and assessment. In M. C. Wittrock & E. L. Baker (Eds.), *Testing and cognition* (pp. 17–30). Englewood Cliffs, NJ: Prentice Hall.

Guion, R. M. (1995). Comments on values and standards in performance assessments. *Educational Measurement: Issues and Practice, 14*(4), 25–27.

Hambleton, R. K. (1997, October). *Promising GMAT item formats for the 21st century.* Invited presentation at the international workshop on the GMAT, Paris, France.

Herl, H. E., O'Neil, H. F., Jr., Chung, G. K. W. K., & Schacter, J. (1999). Reliability and validity of a computer-based knowledge mapping system to measure content understanding. *Computers in Human Behavior, 15,* 315–333.

Huff, K. L., & Sireci, S. G. (2001). Validity issues in computer-based testing. *Educational Measurement: Issues and Practice, 20*(3), 16–25.

Jamieson, J., Taylor, C., Kirsch, I., & Eignor, D. (1998). Design and evaluation of a computer-based TOEFL tutorial. *System, 26,* 485–513.

Jodoin, M. G. (2001, April). *An empirical examination of IRT information for innovative item formats in a computer-based certification testing program.* Paper presented at the annual meeting of the National Council on Measurement in Education, Seattle, WA.

Kane, M. T. (1992). The assessment of professional competence. *Evaluation and the Health Professions, 15,* 163–182.

Kane, M., Crooks, T., & Cohen, A. (1999). Validating measures of performance. *Educational Measurement: Issues and Practice, 18*(2), 5–17.

Kaplan, R. M., & Bennett, R. E. (1994). *Using the free-response scoring tool to automatically score the formulating hypotheses item* (ETS Research Report No. 94–08). Princeton, NJ: Educational Testing Service.

Klein, D. C. D., O'Neil, H. F., Jr., & Baker, E. L. (1998). *A cognitive demands analysis of innovative technologies* (CSE Tech. Rep. No. 454). Los Angeles, CA: UCLA, National Center for Research on Evaluation, Student Standards, and Testing.

Landauer, T. K., Foltz, P. W., & Laham, D. (1998). An introduction to latent semantic analysis. *Discourse Processes, 25,* 259–284.

Landauer, T. K., Laham, D., Rehder, B., & Schreiner, M. E. (1997). How well can passage meaning be derived without using word order? A comparison of latent semantic analysis and humans. In G. Shafto & P. Langley (Eds.), *Proceedings of the 19th annual meeting of the Cognitive Science Society* (pp. 412–417). Mahwah, NJ: Lawrence Erlbaum Associates, Inc.

Larkey, L. S. (1998). *Automatic essay grading using text categorization techniques.* In the Proceedings of the 21st Annual International Conference of the Association for Computing Machinery—Special Interest Group on Information Retrieval, Melbourne, Australia, 90–95.

Linn, R. L., & Burton, E. (1994). Performance-based assessment: Implications of task specificity. *Educational Measurement: Issues and Practice, 13*(1), 5–8, 15.

Luecht, R. M. (2001, April). *Capturing, codifying, and scoring complex data for innovative, computer-based items.* Paper presented at the annual meeting of the National Council on Measurement in Education, Seattle, WA.

Martinez, M. E. (1991). A comparison of multiple-choice and constructed figural response items. *Journal of Educational Measurement, 28,* 131–145.

Martinez, M. E., & Bennett, R. E. (1992). A review of automatically scorable constructed-response item types for large-scale assessment. *Applied Measurement in Education, 5,* 151–169.

Messick, S. (1995). Standards of validity and the validity of standards in performance assessment. *Educational Measurement: Issues and Practice, 14*(4), 5–9.

Microsoft Corporation. (1998, September). *Procedures and guidelines for writing Microsoft Certification Exams.* Redmond, WA: Author.

Mills, C. (2000, February). *Unlocking the promise of CBT.* Keynote address presented at a conference of the Association of Test Publishers, Carmel Valley, CA.

Mislevy, R. J., Steinberg, L. S., Breyer, F. J., Almond, R. G., & Johnson, L. (1999, September 16–17). *Making sense of data from complex assessments.* Paper presented at the 1999 CRESST Conference, Los Angeles, CA.

National Council of Architectural Registration Boards. (2000). *ARE practice program* [Computer software]. Retrieved March 20, 2000, from http://www.ncarb.org/are/tutorial2.html

Nhouyvanisvong, A., Katz, I. R., & Singley, M. K. (1997). *Toward a unified model of problem solving in well-determined and under-determined algebra word problems.* Paper presented at the annual meeting of the American Educational Research Association, Chicago.

O'Neil, K., & Folk, V. (1996, April). *Innovative CBT item formats in a teacher licensing program.* Paper presented at the annual meeting of the National Council on Measurement in Education, New York.

Page, E. B., & Peterson, N. S. (1995). The computer moves into essay grading: Updating the ancient test. *Phi Delta Kappan, 76,* 561–565.

Page, E. B. (1994). Computer grading of student prose, using modern concepts and software. *Journal of Experimental Education, 62*(2), 127–142.

Parshall, C. G., & Balizet, S. (2001). Audio computer-based tests (CBTS): An initial framework for the use of sound in computerized tests. *Educational Measurement: Issues and Practice, 20*(2), 5–15.

Parshall, C. G., Davey, T., & Pashley, P. (2000). Innovative item types for computerized testing. In W. J. van der Linden & C. Glas (Eds.), *Computer-adaptive testing: Theory and practice* (pp. 129–148). Boston: Kluwer Academic.

Rehder, B., Schreiner, M. E., Wolfe, M. B., Laham, D., Landauer, T. K., & Kintsch, W. (1998). Using latent semantic analysis to assess knowledge: Some technical considerations. *Discourse Processes, 25,* 337–354.

Rizavi, S., & Sireci, S.G. (1999). *Comparing computerized and human scoring of WritePlacer Essays* (Laboratory of Psychometric and Evaluative Research Report No. 354). Amherst: School of Education, University of Massachusetts.

Sebrechts, M. M., Bennett, R. E., & Rock, D. A. (1991). Agreement between expert system and human raters' scores on complex constructed-response quantitative items. *Journal of Applied Psychology, 76,* 856–862.

Shavelson, R. J., Baxter, G., & Pine, J. (1991). Performance assessment in science. *Applied Measurement in Education, 4,* 347–362.

Taylor, C., Jamieson, J., Eignor, D., & Kirsch, I. (1998). *The relationship between computer familiarity and performance on computer-based TOEFL test tasks* [ETS Research Rep. No. 98–08]. Princeton, NJ: Educational Testing Service.

van der Linden, W. J., & Hambleton, R. K. (Eds.). (1997). *Handbook of modern item response theory.* New York: Springer.

Vispoel, W. P. (1999). Creating computerized adaptive tests of music aptitude: Problems, solutions, and future directions. In F. Drasgow & J. B. Olson-Buchanan (Eds.), *Innovations in computerized assessment* (pp. 151–176). Mahwah, NJ: Lawrence Erlbaum Associates, Inc.

Walker, G., & Crandall, J. (1999, February). *Value added by computer-based TOEFL test* [TOEFL briefing]. Princeton, NJ: Educational Testing Service.

Williamson, D. M., Bejar, I. I., & Hone, A. S. (1999). 'Mental model' comparisons of automated and human scoring. *Journal of Educational Measurement, 36,* 158–184.

Williamson, D. M., Hone, A. S., Miller, S., & Bejar, I. I. (1998, April). *Classification trees for quality control processes in automated constructed response scoring.* Paper presented at the annual meeting of the National Council on Measurement in Education, San Diego, CA.

Yang, Y., Buckendahl, C. W., Juszkiewicz, P. I., & Bhola, D. S. (2002/this issue). A review of strategies for validating computer automated scoring. *Applied Measurement in Education, 15,* 391–412.

Zenisky, A. L., & Sireci, S. (2001). Feasibility review of selected performance assessment item types for the computerized Uniform CPA Exam (Laboratory of Psychometric and Evaluative Research Rep. No. 405). Amherst: School of Education, University of Massachusetts.

APPLIED MEASUREMENT IN EDUCATION, *15*(4), 363–389

Making Sense of Data
From Complex Assessments

Robert J. Mislevy
University of Maryland
Educational Testing Service

Linda S. Steinberg
Educational Testing Service
Princeton, NJ

F. Jay Breyer
The Chauncey Group International
Princeton, NJ

Russell G. Almond
Educational Testing Service
Princeton, NJ

Lynn Johnson
Dental Interactive Simulations Corporation
Denver, CO

Advances in cognitive psychology both deepen our understanding of how students gain and use knowledge and broaden the range of performances and situations we want to see to acquire evidence about their developing knowledge. At the same time, advances in technology make it possible to capture more complex performances in assessment settings by including, as examples, simulation, interactivity, and extended responses. The challenge is making sense of the complex data that result. This article concerns an evidence-centered approach to the design and analysis of complex assessments. We present a design framework that incorporates integrated structures for a modeling knowledge and skills, designing tasks, and extracting and syn-

Requests for reprints should be sent to Robert J. Mislevy, Benjamin 1230-C, University of Maryland, College Park, MD 20742. E-mail: rmislevy@umd.edu

thesizing evidence. The ideas are illustrated in the context of a project with the Dental Interactive Simulation Corporation (DISC), assessing problem solving in dental hygiene with computer-based simulations. After reviewing the substantive grounding of this effort, we describe the design rationale, statistical and scoring models, and operational structures for the DISC assessment prototype.

Interest in complex and innovative assessment is increasing these days for a number of reasons. For one, we have opportunities to capitalize on recent advances in cognitive and educational psychology: how people learn, how they organize knowledge, how they put it to use (Greeno, Collins, & Resnick, 1997). This broadens the range of what we want to know about students and what we might see to give us evidence (Glaser, Lesgold, & Lajoie, 1987). We have opportunities to put new technologies to use in assessment: to create new kinds of tasks, to bring them to life, to interact with examinees (Bennett, 1999).

But how are we to make sense of data from complex assessments? Don Melnick (1996), who for several years led the National Board of Medical Examiners (NBME) project on computer-based case management problems, observed,

> The NBME has consistently found the challenges in the development of innovative testing methods to lie primarily in the scoring arena. Complex test stimuli result in complex responses, which require complex models to capture and appropriately combine information from the test to create a valid score. (p. 117)

The statistical methods and rules-of-thumb that evolved to manage classroom quizzes and standardized tests often fall short of this goal.

This article is based on two premises. The first is that the tools of probability-based reasoning, which specialize to familiar test theory to model data from familiar forms of testing, can be applied from first principles to model complex data from innovative forms of testing (Mislevy, 1994; Mislevy & Gitomer, 1996). Recent developments in statistics and expert systems make it possible to build models and obtain estimates for more complex situations than were hitherto possible. The second premise is that flexible models and powerful statistical methods alone are not good enough. It is a poor strategy to hope to figure out "how to score it" only after an assessment has been constructed and performances have been captured. Rather, one should design a complex assessment from the very start around the inferences one wants to make, the observations one needs to ground them, the situations that will evoke those observations, and the chain of reasoning that connects them.

To this end, we have been developing an "evidence-centered" framework for designing assessments (Mislevy, Steinberg, & Almond, 2002b). We are using this framework to tackle design and scoring issues for a simulation-based assessment of problem solving in dental hygiene, a project of the Dental Interactive Simulations Corporation (DISC; Johnson et al., 1998). A previous article (Mislevy,

Steinberg, Breyer, Almond, & Johnson, 1999) described the cognitive task analysis that was carried out to provide substantive and psychological grounding for the proposed assessment. This article concerns the next stage in the project—constructing the design objects around which an operational assessment can be built. In the first part of the article we review the design framework and the cognitive task analysis. Next, we describe how the design objects were fleshed out. Particular emphasis is placed on evidence models—reusable substantive and statistical structures that frame the evidentiary argument from observations of complex data to inferences about complex skills. Finally, we outline the ways that the pieces are assembled for assessing examinees in an operational program.

EVIDENCE-CENTERED ASSESSMENT DESIGN

Reasoning From Complex Data

So how should we make sense of data from complex assessments? We may begin by asking how people make sense of complex data more generally. Just how do we reason from masses of data of different kinds, fraught with dependencies, hiding redundancies and contradictions, each addressing different strands of a tangled web of interrelationships? Put simply, humans interpret complex data in terms of some underlying "story." It might be a narrative, an organizing theory, a statistical model, or some combination of many of these. It might be a simplifying schema we can hold in mind all at once, such as "30 days hath September ..." to remember how many days each month has, or a complicated structure, such as a compendium of blueprints for a skyscraper. This is how we reason in law, in medicine, in weather forecasting, in everyday life (Schum, 1994). We weave some sensible and defensible story around the specifics: a story that addresses what we really care about, at a higher level of generality and a more basic level of concern than any of the particulars. A story that builds around what we believe to be the fundamental principles and patterns in the domain. In law, for example, every case is unique, but jurists use statutes, precedents, and recurring themes from the human experience as building blocks to understand each new case (Pennington & Hastie, 1991).

The building blocks of evidentiary reasoning we must use to connect what we know about a substantive domain with what we see in the world are equally important. Research in cognitive decision making suggests that certain patterns seem to be "wired in" to people to use as building blocks for reasoning—heuristics such as estimating prevalence from familiarity, and causation from co-occurrence. Wired-in, generally useful, and sometimes dead wrong (Kahneman, Slovic, & Tversky, 1982). Gardner (1991) argued that in any discipline, building blocks derived from principled understandings of "the way things really work" are hard won for just this reason.

Insights into evidentiary reasoning in a general form—that is, patterns and principles that apply across many domains, each working with its own underlying substance and forms of evidence—have appeared over the years in fields as varied as philosophy, jurisprudence, statistics, and computer science. The approach we take next can be viewed as the application of the general approach espoused by Schum (1994): structuring arguments from evidence to inference in terms of generating principles in the domain, and using probability-based reasoning to manage uncertainty (see also Pellegrino, Chudowsky, & Glaser, 2001).

Evidentiary Reasoning and Assessment Design

In educational assessment, the building blocks of the stories that connect what students know and can do with what students say and actually do come from the nature of reasoning in assessment and the nature of the learning in the domain in question. The previously mentioned evidence-centered design project provides a conceptual framework for designing assessments in this light. In this article we draw on the perspective and a high-level description of the central objects and interrelationships. This section sets the stage by laying out the basic structure of what we have called a *conceptual assessment framework*, or CAF. Then we discuss in greater detail how the ideas play out in the DISC prototype assessment.

Figure 1 is a high-level schematic of the three basic models we suggest must be present, and must be coordinated, to achieve a coherent assessment. They are student models, evidence models, and task models. A quote from Messick (1994) serves well to introduce them:

> A construct-centered approach [to assessment design] would begin by asking what complex of knowledge, skills, or other attribute should be assessed, presumably because they are tied to explicit or implicit objectives of instruction or are otherwise valued by society. Next, what behaviors or performances should reveal those constructs, and what tasks or situations should elicit those behaviors? Thus, the nature of the construct guides the selection or construction of relevant tasks as well as the rational development of construct-based scoring criteria and rubrics. (p. 17)

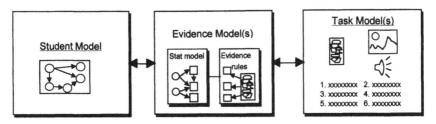

FIGURE 1   Three basic models of assessment design.

The Student Model

What complex of knowledge, skills, or other attributes should be assessed? This is what the student model is about. Configurations of values of student model variables (SM variables) are meant to approximate certain aspects of the infinite configurations of skill and knowledge real students have, as seen from some perspective about skill and knowledge in the domain. It could be the perspective of behaviorist, trait, cognitive, or situative psychology. This perspective determines the kinds of stories we want to weave for our purposes, but the evidentiary problem of constructing them from limited evidence is essentially the same. These are the terms in which we want to talk about students—the level at which we build our story, to determine evaluations, make decisions, or plan instruction. But we do not see the values directly. We just see what the students say or do, and we must construe that as evidence about the SM variables.

In addition to one's conception of competence in the domain, the number and nature of the SM variables in a particular application also depend on the purpose of the assessment. A single variable characterizing overall proficiency might suffice in an assessment meant to support only a summary pass–fail decision; a coached practice system that helps students develop the same proficiency would require a finer grained student model for monitoring how a student is doing on particular aspects of skill and knowledge for which we can provide feedback.

The student model in Figure 1 depicts SM variables as circles. The arrows connecting them represent important empirical or theoretical associations among them. We use a statistical model to manage our knowledge about a given student's unobservable values for these variables at any given point in time, expressing it as a probability distribution that can be updated in light of new evidence. In particular, the student model takes the form of a fragment of a Bayesian inference network, or Bayes net (see Jensen, 1996, for an introduction to Bayes net from a statistical perspective; Edwards, 1998, for a modeling perspective; and Mislevy, 1994, and Almond & Mislevy, 1999, for an assessment perspective). The Appendix gives a simple example of how one can use the framework of Bayes nets to manage knowledge and uncertainty in assessment. We look more closely at their use in the DISC example provided next.

Evidence Models

What behaviors or performances should reveal those constructs, and what is the connection? This is what evidence models are about. An evidence model is the heart of evidentiary reasoning in assessment. Here is where we lay out our argument about why and how our observations in a given task situation constitute evidence about SM variables.

Figure 1 shows that there are two parts to the evidence model. The *evaluative submodel* concerns extracting the salient features of whatever the student says, does, or creates in the task situation—that is, the *work product*. The work product is represented by a rectangle containing a jumble of complicated figures at the far right of the evidence model. It is a unique human production, perhaps as simple as a mark on a machine-readable answer sheet, perhaps as complex as repeated cycles of evaluation and treatment in a patient-management problem. Three squares are shown coming out of the work product. They represent *observable variables*, or evaluative summaries of whatever the assessment designer has determined are the key aspects of the performance to take away from the performance as nuggets of evidence. The evaluative rules say how to carry out these mappings from unique human actions into a common interpretative framework. This is where one lays out the argument about what is important in a performance, in light of the purpose of the assessment. These mappings can be as simple as determining whether the mark on a multiple-choice answer sheet is the correct answer or as complex as an expert's holistic evaluation of four key aspects of an unconstrained patient–management solution. They can be automatic or they can require human judgment, or some combination of both.

The *statistical submodel* of the evidence model expresses the how the observable variables depend, in probability, on SM variables. This is where one lays out the argument for synthesizing evidence across multiple tasks or from different performances. Figure 1 shows that the observables are modeled as depending on some subset of the SM variables. Examples of models in which values of observed variables depend probabilistically on unobservable variables are classical test theory, item response theory, latent class models, and factor analysis. We can express these familiar models as special cases of Bayes nets and extend the ideas as appropriate to the nature of the SM and observable variables (Almond & Mislevy, 1999; Mislevy, 1994; Mislevy, Wilson, Erkican, & Chudowsky, in press).

Task Models

What tasks or situations should elicit those behaviors? This is what task models are about. A task model provides a framework for constructing and describing the situations in which examinees act. Task model variables (TM variables) play many roles in assessment, including systematizing task construction, focusing the evidentiary value of tasks, guiding assessment assembly, implicitly defining SM variables, and conditioning the statistical argument between observations and SM variables (Mislevy, Steinberg, & Almond, 2002a). A task model includes specifications for the environment in which the student will say, do, or produce something—for example, characteristics of stimulus material, instructions, help, tools, affordances. It also includes specifications for the work product, or the form in which what the student says, does, or produces will be captured. Data from a given task can only be analyzed with a given evidence model if the output work product specifications in the task model that generated the task match the evidence model's input work product specifications.

THE DISC PROJECT

Background

In 1990 a consortium of dental education, licensure, and professional organizations created the DISC to develop computerized assessments and continuing education products that simulate the work dentists and dental hygienists perform in practice (Johnson et al., 1998). The consortium directed DISC to develop, as an initial application, a computer-based performance assessment of problem solving and decision making in dental hygiene. This assessment would fill a gap in the licensure sequence. Hygienists provide preventive and therapeutic dental hygiene services, including educating patients about oral hygiene; examining the head, neck, and oral cavity; and performing prophylaxes, scaling, and root planing. Currently, multiple-choice examinations probe hygienists' content knowledge as it is required in these roles, and clinical examinations assess their skill in carrying out the procedures. But neither form of assessment provides direct evidence about the processes that unfold as hygienists interact with patients: seeking and integrating information from multiple sources, planning dental hygiene treatments accordingly, evaluating the results over time, and modifying treatment plans in light of outcomes or new information.

As this article is written, DISC has developed a prototype of a dental simulation system in the context of continuing education (Johnson et al., 1998). The simulator uses information from a virtual-patient database as a candidate works through a case. Some of the information is presented directly to the candidate (e.g., a medical history questionnaire). Other information may be presented on request (e.g., radiographs at a given point in the case). Still other information is used to compute patient status dynamically as a function of the candidate's actions and the patient's etiology. A student can thus work through interactions with virtual patients—gathering information, planning and carrying out treatments, evaluating their effectiveness. These capabilities provide a starting point for the proposed simulation-based dental hygiene licensure assessment.

Educational Testing Service, under a subcontract with the Chauncey Group International, worked with DISC to develop a "scoring engine" for the proposed prototype of a simulation-based assessment of problem solving in dental hygiene. As stated in the introduction, we believe this requires a broader perspective than just looking for a statistical model to make sense of whatever data happens to appear, from whatever tasks and interfaces happen to have been produced. We therefore worked through student, evidence, and task models with DISC and subsequently examined the implications for the simulation system. These CAF models provide the foundation on which we assemble the building blocks of our evidentiary arguments. The substance of the arguments concerns on the nature of knowledge in dental hygiene, how it can be evidenced, and what is needed to serve the purpose of the DISC assessment.

The following section sketches the assessment framework we developed for the proposed assessment, showing how its elements depend on and are derived from the models of the CAF. The section after that reviews substantive grounding of the project, including the cognitive task analysis. Further discussion of the structure and contents of the design elements then follows.

Design Rationale

The Cognitive Task Analysis

A group of dental hygiene experts assembled by DISC—the DISC Scoring Team—began by mapping out the roles and contexts of the work that dental hygienists perform, drawing on curricular materials, research literature, existing licensure tests, and personal experience. These materials also constituted a compendium of declarative knowledge that would ground both the design of the cognitive task analysis (CTA), as described next, and subsequent developmental work, such as defining TM variables and their values.

A traditional job analysis focuses on valued tasks in a domain, in terms of how often people must perform them and how important they are. A CTA, in contrast, focuses on the knowledge people use to carry out those tasks. A CTA in a given domain seeks to shed light on (a) essential features of the situations, (b) internal representations of situations, (c) the relationship between problem-solving behavior and internal representation, (d) how the problems are solved, and (e) what makes problems hard (Newell & Simon, 1972). With creating assessment schemas as our objective, we adapted cognitive task analysis methods from the expertise literature (Ericcson & Smith, 1991) to capture and to analyze the performance of hygienists at different levels of expertise, under standard conditions, across a range of valued tasks. Details of the CTA appear in Mislevy, Steinberg, Breyer, Almond, and Johnson (1999) and Cameron et al. (1999). The work can be summarized as follows.

Working from the compendium of resources, the scoring team created nine representative cases that require making decisions and solving problems and would be likely to elicit different behavior from hygienists at different levels of proficiency. To produce stimulus materials for the cases, the team began with blank dental forms and charts commonly found in oral health care settings and a corpus of oral photographs, enlarged radiographs, and dental charts of anonymous patients.

We gathered talk-aloud solutions from about 10 hygienists at each of three levels of expertise: novices, or students midway through training; competent hygienists, who recently received their licenses; and acknowledged experts, each of whom has had several years of experience in practice and most of whom also teach in dental education programs. A participant, an expert scoring team member, and one or two psychologist researchers participated in each interview. The expert dental hygienist provided the brief prepared verbal description of the patient in each case in turn. The researcher asked the participant to describe her thoughts aloud and say what she would do next. As the participant progressed through the case, she called for printed information; asked questions; and made assessment, treatment, patient education, and evaluation decisions. With each action, the expert interviewer provided responses in the form of medical or dental history charts, radiographic, photographic, or graphic representations when available, or verbal descriptions of what the patient would say or what the result of a procedure would be. The researcher asked the participant to interpret the information—for example, to say what she thought in reaction to the stimulus, what it might mean, what hypotheses it might have sparked, or which further procedures it might indicate. The interviewers did not give feedback as to the underlying etiology of a case, the appropriateness of the participant's actions, or the accuracy of her responses. The interview continued until the presenting problem was resolved.

Performance Features

The scoring team's mission was to abstract, from the unique and specific actions of 31 individual participants in nine particular cases, general characterizations of patterns of behavior—a language that could describe solutions across participants and cases not only in the data at hand but also in the domain of dental hygiene decision-making problems more broadly. In line with the goal of assessment, the team sought patterns that would be useful in distinguishing hygienists at different levels of competence. We refer to the resulting characterizations as *performance features* (Table 1). We provide these examples:

• Using disparate sources of information: Novice hygienists were usually able to note important cues on particular forms of information, such as shadows on radiographs and bifurcations on probing charts, but they often failed to generate hypotheses that required integrating cues across different forms.

• Scripting behavior: Novice hygienists often followed standard "scripts" to work through initial assessments and patient education, whereas more experienced hygienists increasingly tailored their actions to the conditions and characteristics of specific patients.

• Investigation of hypotheses: Expert performance was generally characterized by pursuing information where it leads. As in many other domains reported in the expertise literature, "some of the protocols show [novices] less able to efficiently modify a schema in response to new data, in contrast to the experts, who were flexibly opportunistic, neither too fixated not uncontrollably labile" (Lesgold

TABLE 1
Performance Features

Features that apply across all phases of the patient treatment cycle

---

Gathering and using information
   Searching for information
   Comparing/contrasting information of a given type over time
   Synthesizing information across disparate types
   Using other resources and information sources
Formulating problems and investigating hypotheses
   Problem formulation
   Investigating hypotheses
Dealing with ethical and legal considerations
   Communication and language
     Adapting language to patient
     Using domain vocabulary in gathering, using, and transmitting information
Scripting behavior

Features that apply to particular phases of the patient treatment cycle

---

Patient assessment
   Degree of planning before carrying out a procedure
   Relating medical history to dental conditions
   Adaptation to complicating medical conditions
   Adaptation to performance situations (e.g., time constraint, nervous patient)
   Adequacy of taking patient history
   Adequacy of medical history procedure
   Addressing the patient's chief complaint
   Adequacy of oral assessment
   Adequacy of periodontal assessment
   Adequacy of radiographic assessment
Adequacy of dental assessment
Treatment planning
   Scripting behavior
   Adequacy of treatment planning
   Appropriateness of referring
Patient education
Scripting behavior
Adequacy of explanation for dental referral
Patient evaluation
   Particular emphasis on "Gathering and using information" and "Formulating problems and
     investigating hypotheses" features listed previously.

---

et al., 1988, p. 319). For competent dental hygienists, investigating hypotheses is often accomplished only partially. Novice dental hygienists frequently do not investigate hypotheses. If they recognize that a problem exists, they may ask another professional to investigate it (not a bad thing in itself!) at an earlier stage than more experienced hygienists, who would gather further information to refine, confirm, or disconfirm early hypotheses.

Design Objects

The patterns summarized as performance features are cognitively grounded indicators of developing expertise in the domain of dental hygiene (Glaser et al., 1987). This is what we want to build the assessment around. What are their implications for constructing the design objects—namely, student, evidence, and task models?

The Student Model

The key considerations for determining a student model are that the SM variables should be consistent with both the results of CTA and the purpose of the assessment. In the case of the DISC prototype assessment, we ask more specifically, What aspects of skill and knowledge might be used to accumulate evidence across tasks, to summarize for pass–fail reporting and to offer finer grained feedback? We drew up a number of possible models. Figure 2 is a slightly simplified version of the final model.

Figure 2 depicts a Bayes net that contains just the SM variables. We refer to it as the student model Bayes net fragment. It is combined with fragments that include observable variables when we need to update our beliefs about the SM variables when data arrive. The SM variables in Figure 2 are represented as ovals. As examples, two toward the upper right are *Assessment*, which concerns proficiency in assessing the status of a new patient, and *Information gathering/Usage*, which concerns proficiency in gathering and using information about patients. The full model (not shown) further elaborates the second of these, distinguishing knowing

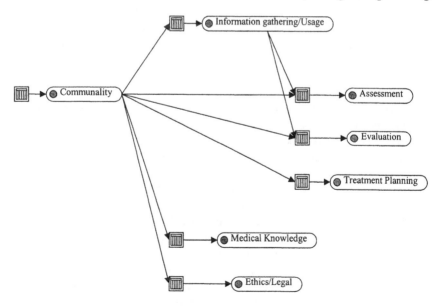

FIGURE 2   Simplified Dental Interactive Simulations Corporation student model.

how and where to obtain information, being able to generate hypotheses that would guide searches and interpretations, and knowing how to gather information that would help confirm or refute hypotheses.

In front of each variable is square that represents the probability distribution that expresses current belief about a student's (unobservable) standing on it. In this application, each variable is defined as having three levels—low, medium, and high—which correspond to novice, competent, and expert status. The arrows indicate associations among the variables; specifically, conditional dependence relationships. A hygienist who has high proficiency in gathering and using information, for example, is likely to have high or at least medium proficiency in assessing the initial status of new patients. The *Communality* SM variable is a mechanism for incorporating the belief that the finely grained aspects of dental hygiene proficiency are probably correlated in the target population of examinees. Even if our interest lies at the more detailed level, allowing for associations serves two useful purposes. First, we can exploit direct evidence about one aspect as indirect evidence about another. Second, if DISC wishes to project the finer grained SM variables to a summary scale for a pass–fail decision, modeling their associations permits us to calculate measures of accuracy of such functions.

At the beginning of an examinee's assessment, the probability distributions representing a new student's status will be relatively uninformative—perhaps an empirical estimate of the distribution in a population the examinee to which belongs, perhaps a very diffuse prior so beliefs will reflect evidence from her actions almost exclusively. In the following sections we discuss how we successively update the joint distribution of the SM variables to reflect our changing belief as we make observations. Evidence models provide the technical machinery for making these changes, in accordance with the evidentiary argument that justifies them.

Evidence Models

The SM variables represent the proficiencies in which our interest lies, but they are inherently unobservable. The Appendix shows with a simple example how one uses Bayes nets to update beliefs about unobservable proficiency variables, using evidence in the form of values of observable variables. What might be useful observable variables in this dental hygiene application? And what might be prototypical structures for getting evidence in these forms to tell us about students' proficiencies—structures around which many individual cases can be constructed?

The CTA produced performance features that characterize patterns of behavior and differentiate levels of expertise. They are grist for generally defined, reusable observed variables in evidence models. The evidence models themselves are structured assemblies of SM variables and observable variables, including general rules for determining the values of the observable variables and updating SM variables accordingly. We defined 33 reusable evidence models for use with potential DISC cases. Examples of the situations they address are "Hypothesis testing in patient assessment," "Treatment planning, with a legal/ethical issue," and "Information gathering in patient evaluation, with a medical complication." As described later, a particular case utilizes the structures of one or more evidence models, fleshed out in accordance with specifics of that case.

Figure 3 depicts the Bayes net fragment that comprises the statistical submodel of one particular evidence model we use to discuss the building-block aspect of evidentiary reasoning. It concerns gathering patient information when assessing a new patient's status, in the absence of inherent ethical or medical complications. We use it to show how evidence models are built from reusable structural elements, then tailored to the specifics of individual cases.

At the far left, there are SM variables we posit to drive performance in these situations: *Assessment* of new patients and *Information gathering /Usage*, the two that were highlighted in the discussion of the student model. The *Context* variable at the lower left accounts for dependencies among different aspects of performance in the same setting, to avoid "double-counting" evidence that arises as different aspects of the same performance. The nodes on the right are generally defined observable variables. Two of them are how well the examinee succeeds at *adapting to situational constraints* and *adequacy of examination procedures* in terms of how well their rationale is grounded. All the observable variables are defined as having between two and five possible values, generally ordered from poor to high quality. Adequacy of examination procedures, for example, has three values: *All* of the necessary points of an appropriate rationale are present in the examinee's solution, *some* are present, or *none* or few are present. These are generic categories that are particularized for actual specific cases, the part of the evidentiary argument that is addressed in the evaluation submodel.

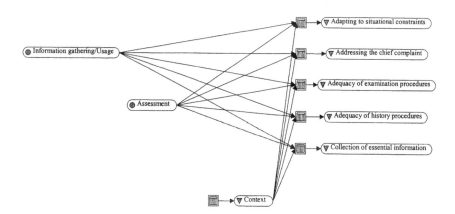

FIGURE 3   The Bayes net fragment in an evidence model.

The evaluation submodel.   As mentioned previously, the evaluation sub-model of an evidence model concerns the mappings from unique human actions or productions into a common framework of evaluation (i.e., from work products to values of observable variables). Many tasks can be built around the same evidence model because the structure of the evidentiary argument is essentially the same.

There are constants in the evaluation submodels for tasks that are built to conform with the same evidence model: (a) the identification and formal definition of observable variables and (b) generally stated "proto-rules" for evaluating their values. Adequacy of examination procedure is an aspect of any assessment of any new patient, for example; we can define a generally stated evaluative framework to describe how well an examinee has adapted to whatever situation is presented in terms of, say, a three-valued ordered variable with the following values: *high*, or adequate grounding for examination procedures; *medium*, or partial grounding of procedures; and *low*, or inadequate grounding.

What is customized to particular cases are case-specific rules for evaluating values of observables—tailored instantiations of the proto-rules that address the specifics of case. The unique features of a particular virtual patient's initial presentation in a given assessment situation determine what an examinee should do in assessment and why. Experts must then specify the features of the content and rationale of examinees' assessment procedures that will determine the mapping to high, medium, and low values for this observable variable.

The "Mr. Clay" case, for example, requires gathering information to assess the status of a new patient. Given the specifics of the setup and the information about Mr. Clay, experts determined that an examinee should base examination procedures on two grounds: his chief complaint and the exception items on his health history review. A rationale having both grounds gets mapped to the high value, a rationale with just one gets mapped to medium, and a rationale with neither gets mapped to the low value.

The statistical submodel.   The statistical submodel of an evidence model concerns the synthesis of evidence from multiple or different tasks (arriving in the form of values of observable variables), in terms of our evolving beliefs about SM variables. It consists of the structure and the conditional probabilities in a Bayes net fragment, as seen in Figure 3.

There are constants in the statistical submodels of tasks that are built around the same evidence model: (a) the identities of the student model parents, (b) the identities of the observable variables, and (c) the structure of the conditional probability relationships between the student model parents and their observable children. For example, proficiency in information gathering/usage and assessment of new patients is required to have high probabilities of adequately grounding assessment procedures in any case that involves assessing a new patient.

Certain things are customized to particular cases: (a) the specific meanings of the observables, through the case-specific evaluation rules discussed previously, and (b) the values of the conditional probabilities that specify how potential outcomes depend on the values of SM variables. Are the constraints imposed for this Virtual Patient A quite straightforward, for example so that even novices are likely to adapt to them? Are the constraints for Virtual Patient B subtle but demanding so that even experts are not likely to make all of the ideal accommodations? The values of the conditional probabilities can be approximated initially from expert opinion and knowledge about the specific features of the task. Empirical data can be used to refine the estimates, much as we estimate the parameters in item response theory models (Mislevy, Almond, Yan, & Steinberg, 1999).

Accumulating evidence.   SM variables and observable variables play asymmetric roles when we assess an examinee. Our interest in the (unobservable) values of the examinee's SM variables is persistent. We want to make decisions and provide feedback based on their values as we learn about them from her performance across a series of tasks. The values of the observables that her task performances produce are of interest because they allow us to update our beliefs about her SM variables. Here is what happens during the course of observation: We start with a student model with probability distributions that indicate we know very little about this new examinee. We administer a case, and as the examinee works through the phases of the encounter, we successively "dock" a sequence of appropriate evidence models to incorporate information from her performances (Almond, Herkskovits, Mislevy, & Steinberg, 1999). Each time, we use the evidence model structure to integrate information from the situation at hand into the probability distributions for the SM variables.

The evidence model we have been looking at has two SM variables we posited to drive probabilities of actions in a certain class of situations. These variables are the link between the evidence model Bayes net fragment and the student model Bayes net fragment. Encountering a task situation for which this evidence model is appropriate, we construct a combined Bayes net from the student model Bayes net fragment and the evidence model Bayes net fragment (Figure 4). We parse the work product and evaluate the observed variables. We enter these values in this combined Bayes net and update our beliefs about the SM variables.

Figure 5 provides a numerical example from using a representation that shows probability distributions for each variable. The evidence model discussed previously is shown docked to the student model. The probabilities illustrate belief after observing high-quality values on four observable variables that can be evaluated from the work product, from an uninformative prior distribution. The values for one observable variable are shown in the box at the right; they show a probability of 1 for the value that was actually observed and zero for the other two. The probabilities in the SM variable for assessment proficiency have, appropriately, shifted

Student Model Fragment   Evidence Model Fragment

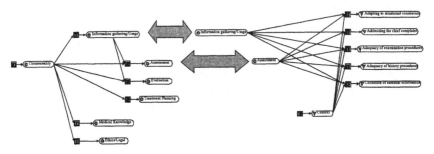

Combined Bayes net

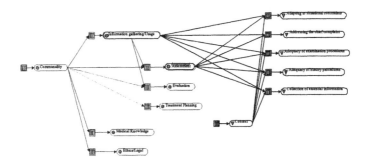

FIGURE 4   Docking student model and evidence model Bayes net fragments.

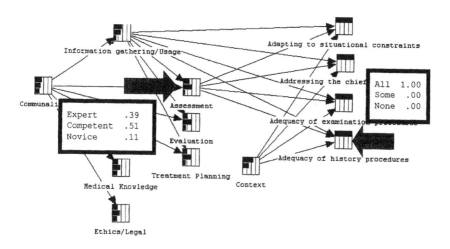

FIGURE 5   Numerical representations of status after four "good" findings.

upward. Having made these observations and registering the impact on our beliefs, we can jettison the Bayes net fragment for this evidence model—keeping the student model fragment, with its updated probability distributions—and move to the next phase of the case or to a different case, or stop testing and report results.

The DISC Scoring Engine allows DISC to specify arbitrary functions of SM variables to obtain summary scores and accompanying measures of precision, based on the final or any intermediate state of the student model distribution. The Next Steps section has a bit more to say about these functions.

Task Models

Task models are the building blocks for the situations in which we make observations. Task models, one can recall, are schemas for describing and creating the situations that evoke the actions we need to see so we can determine values for those observable variables in the evidence models. For the DISC prototype, we need to define TM variables that

- the simulator needs for the virtual-patient database.
- characterize features that evoke specified aspects of skill and knowledge.
- characterize features of tasks that affect their difficulty.
- characterize features we need to assemble tasks into tests.

This section gives examples of TM variables with an eye toward these functions.

To anticipate one of the key ideas from the Putting the Pieces Together section, a test developer can create a case by first referring to the Proficiency/Evidence/Task (P/E/T) matrix. The P/E/T matrix is a cross-referenced list of the SM variables, evidence models that can be used to get information about each of them, and task models around which tasks can be constructed that furnish values for the observables in those evidence models. Once a task model is selected, it is fleshed out with particulars to create a new virtual patient. The values of all the TM variables used in that task model are determined accordingly.

There are distinguishable groups of TM variables, many of which are hierarchically related. For example, *oral hygiene status* is a TM variable with possible values (excellent, good, poor, extremely poor). Another TM variable that is part of oral hygiene status is *bacterial plaque*, which has possible values (Stage 1, Stage 2, Stage 3, heavy, moderate, light, none); *plaque location* is part of bacterial plaque in turn and indicates where the plaque, if it is present, is found. *Periodontal status* is a very important variable. Nested within it are TM variables *gingival status-attached* and *-marginal*, and within each of them, variables for *color, probing depth, contour,* and *size.* Values for the most detailed level include both "within normal limits" (WNL) and various classes of irregularities that can be used as cues for underlying etiologies. The presence and severity of values other than WNL determine values of the higher level variables such as periodontal status.

Examples of TM variables that concern the setting of the case are *appointment factors* (which nests *number of visits*, *type of visit*, and *time between appointments*) and *documentation status* (which nests *documentation age*, *documentation familiarity*, *documentation completeness*, and *documentation availability*). The documentation status variables are important in providing evidence about certain aspects of examinees' proficiencies in obtaining information. If we want to learn about an examinee's ability to seek and interpret information that can be obtained but is not initially present, then we cannot have documentation completeness set at "all information presented."

TM variables that describe the patient include, as examples, *age*, *sex*, *last visit*, *reason for last visit*, *weight*, *odors*, *symptoms of abuse/neglect*, *demeanor*, and *risk for medical emergency*. Some of these are required for choosing stimulus material, such as photographs of the patient and responses to medical and personal background questions. Others are important for focusing evidence. Risk for medical emergency, for example, should be set to *low* or *none* for cases in which evidence about *medical knowledge* is not sought, but values of *moderate* or *high* necessitate the use of evidence models that do include medical knowledge as student model parents. These variables also play roles in determining the mix of cases to present to examinees. Every assessment might be required to include at exactly one geriatric patient and one pediatric patient, for example, and the same number of male and female patients.

Characteristics of anticipated solutions are another important group of TM variables. *Cues per solution*, for example, indicates the complexity of a case that involves assessment or evaluation; it takes a value of "one" for simple cases, "few" for a moderately complex case, and "many" for a challenging case. TM variables like this help determine conditional probabilities in the Bayes net for a case, either in informing expert judgments or as collateral information when estimating the probabilities from data. *Periodontal assessment procedures* contains a vector of procedures that can be carried out and indicates which are "essential," "indicated," "irrelevant," and "contraindicated." This vector of values, determined by the task developer with expert advice, grounds evaluation rules for observables that concern treatment planning.

When a case uses a given task model, all the TM variables associated with that case must be assigned values. The list may be long, but setting the values need not be arduous. Some TM variables are functions of lower level variables. *Case complexity* is a higher level TM variable that is useful for modeling task difficulty and for assembling tests; its value is derived from lower level TM variables that indicate the specifics of the virtual-patient's condition. Lower level TM variables can be assigned default values based on typical distributions of "normal variation" given basic conditions such as patient age and sex. Determining an underlying condition can imply constellations of expected values for many lower level TM variables. These relationships could be automated in an authoring system that would allow the test developer to focus on exception conditions.

Besides TM variables, task models include specifications for work products. The DISC simulator provides the sequence of actions an examinee makes, sometimes called a transaction list or an event trace. The task model describes its format and the code for its contents, including markers for phases of a case that can be used to signal the need for appropriate evidence models. When an examinee responds to a case, a work product that meets these specifications and contains the specifics of her actions is produced. In turn it will be parsed and evaluated by the evidence rules in the appropriate evidence models. Work product specifications defined in the task model thus link the simulator at one end (the simulator must be capable of producing a product of this form) and evidence models at the other end (the parsing rules in an evidence model expect a work product with a predefined format and kinds of content). They illustrate how carefully defining assessment design objects up front coordinates the work of very different kinds of experts, in this instance simulator designers and dental hygienists.

The CTA suggested the value of some additional, more structured, work products. The scoring team found consistent distinctions among novice, competent, and expert hygienists in not only the actions they chose but also the reasons they gave for choosing them. Many of the performance features concerned intermediate mental products such as identifying cues, generating hypotheses, and selecting tests to explore conjectures—steps often not manifest in actual practice but which directly involve the central knowledge and skills of problem solving in dental hygiene. To capture more direct evidence of this thinking than can be inferred from a transaction list alone, DISC will use work products that require the examinee to make normally mental steps explicit. Information-gathering actions during patient assessment and evaluation will need to be justified by specific hypotheses or as standard of care for the situation, and hypotheses will need to be justified by cues from available forms of information (in formats using nested lists of standard dental hygiene terms and procedures). Following patient assessment and evaluation, summary forms that require synthesizing findings will need to be completed (in a format similar to those of the insurance forms now integral to the practice of dental hygiene).

The Simulator

It may seem ironic that in an article about a simulation-based assessment the shortest section is the one on the simulator itself. There are two reasons for this. The lesser is that other sources of information about the DISC simulator are already available, Johnson et al. (1998) chief among them. The more important reason is our desire to emphasize the evidentiary foundation that must be laid if we are to make sense of any complex assessment data. The central issues concern construct definition, forms of evidence, and situations that can provide evidence, regardless of the means by which data are to be gathered and evaluated. Technology provides possibilities, such as simulation-based scenarios, but these evidentiary considerations shape the thousands of decisions about how technologies can serve the purpose of the assessment.

In the case of DISC, the simulator needs to be able to create the task situations described in the task model, and to capture that behavior in a form we have determined we need to obtain evidence about targeted knowledge—that is, to produce the required work products. What possibilities, constraints, and affordances must be built into simulator to provide the data we need? As to the kinds of situations that will evoke the behavior we want to see, the simulator must be able to

- present the distinct phases in the patient interaction cycle (assessment, treatment planning, treatment implementation, and evaluation).
- present the forms of information that are typically used and control their availability and accessibility so we can learn about examinees' information-gathering skills.
- manage cross time cases versus single visits so we can get evidence about examinees' capabilities to evaluate information over time.
- vary the virtual patient's state dynamically so we can learn about examinees' ability to evaluate the outcomes of treatments that she chooses.

As to the nature of affordances that must be provided, DISC has learned from the CTA that examinees should have the capacity to

- seek and gather data.
- indicate hypotheses.
- justify hypotheses with respect to cues.
- justify actions with respect to hypotheses.

A key point is that DISC does not take the early version of the simulator as given and fixed. Ultimately, the simulator must be designed so the highest priority is providing evidence about the targeted skills and knowledge—not authenticity, not look and feel, not technology. (Messick's, 1994, discussion on designing performance assessments is mandatory reading in this regard.)

Putting the Pieces Together

In the previous sections we first reviewed a general schema for the evidentiary framework of complex assessments and then showed how the necessary building blocks are constructed around the substance and purpose of a particular domain and a particular product. In this section we describe how the pieces are fashioned and assembled in an operational assessment by giving an overview of the DISC assessment design framework and scoring engine.

Creating Tasks

The key to knowing how to score complex tasks is designing them so you know they can evoke evidence about targeted knowledge and skills in ways you will be able to recognize, and know how to accumulate.

The first step in establishing a framework for task creation is fleshing out the student, evidence, and task models in accordance with the substance of the domain and the purposes of the assessment. TM variables are used in any of the task models for describing features of tasks that are important to focus evidence, determine difficulty, ensure domain coverage, and so on (see Mislevy, Steinberg, & Almond, 2002a) on the roles of TM variables. They are cataloged as a common reference for task developers. The P/E/T matrix is a cross-referenced list derived from the models. A task developer who wants to write a task that taps a particular aspect of proficiency can check this matrix to learn what observable variables are available to provide evidence about it and which task models can be used to construct tasks that provide values for these observables.

DISC "tasks" would be defined at a level compatible with distinguishable phases of interactions with patients—that is, initial patient assessment, treatment planning, treatment implementation, and follow-up evaluation. There can be more than one iteration of this cycle. A DISC case can therefore comprise more than one task. The following process is carried out for each. Having decided on a certain task model, the developer instantiates the particulars that will make a unique task. This involves determining values of the TM variables that are involved in tasks written to this task model and finding or creating suitable stimulus materials. The *form* of the work products will have been laid out in the work product specifications of the chosen task model, but their specifics now need to be determined. The developer may need to work with domain experts at this point to determine the features of solutions, ideal and not so ideal, which will form the basis of case-specific evaluation rules. The DISC patient database describes this case for the simulator. It contains the values of the TM variables and the stimulus materials, specified as required to present and control the task in the DISC simulator environment, along with designation of the task model(s) and pointers to evidence models that will be needed in scoring performances.

Calibrating Tasks

Cases are written within the frameworks that task and evidence models provide, as described previously. The statistical submodel of the evidence model contains the structure of the appropriate Bayes net fragment but not conditional probability distributions that are tailored to its particulars. That is, is it harder or easier than typical cases written with the same evidentiary skeleton and does it provide a bit more or less evidence about the various SM variables it informs? To some degree these conditional probabilities can be based on expert knowledge and on previous empirical results from other tasks. More formally, we can estimate the conditional distributions from pretest data, or field trials of the cases.

We consider estimating the conditional probabilities of a new case, say the "Ms. Barlow" case, when it is possible to collect data for both it and one or more previously calibrated cases. Mislevy, Almond, Yan, and Steinberg (1999) and Mislevy et al. (in press) provided technical discussions of this process; what follows is a nontechnical summary.

The structure and the initial values for conditional probabilities are available for the student model and the new case. The case may require multiple Bayes net fragment if it moves through multiple stages of interaction with the patient. Also available are conditional probabilities specific to the previously calibrated cases being presented, and field test data for all the cases from a sample of examinees. The conditional distributions for the new case can then be estimated. Conditional distributions for the previously calibrated tasks and for the student population can be refined as well at this stage if desired. The conditional probabilities for the new task are linked to it. With the particular values of its TM variables, its case-specific evidence rules, and now case-specific conditional probabilities, it is ready to use in estimating the proficiencies of new examinees.

Scoring an Examinee's Performance

In the preceding sections we sketched the processes of task creation and calibration. They are prerequisites to assessing individual examinees—that is, presenting them with cases, gathering evidence about their knowledge and skills, and synthesizing this information in terms of the targeted proficiencies. An overview of the scoring process follows; again the interested reader is referred to Mislevy, Almond, Yan, and Steinberg (1999).

The simulator references an algorithm that guides selection and sequencing of cases. A particular case that has been developed using the evidentiary framework is presented in the DISC simulation environment. The user's solution to a case is captured by the DISC simulator in the form of one or more task-specific work products. "Scoring" of performance on a case begins as the work products produced by the examinee through the DISC simulator are examined for their evidentiary content. This is accomplished by processing each work product with task-specific rules of evidence. These rules of evidence evaluate a work product for the presence, absence, count, and quality of a predefined set of solution characteristics, or observable variables. This analysis produces a specific value for all observables associated with the task for which data are available in the work product.

Once the body of evidence from a case is represented as realized values of observables, it is ready to be absorbed into the DISC Student Model. At this point, the DISC Student Model contains a probability distribution representing what is currently known about the user, possibly reflecting evidence that has been absorbed from previous cases. The DISC Scoring Engine per se consists of the DISC Student Model, predefined sets of observable variables with established relationships to SM variables (the structures of the evidence model Bayes net fragments), and evidence integration routines. The DISC Scoring Engine also provides for general-purpose functions that operate on the student model distribution to calculate the values of customer-specified summary scores and measures of their precision.

CONCLUSION

What is the payoff we hope to gain from all this work? Basically, a framework for creating an indefinite series of unique realistic cases, each complex and interactive—but for each of which, we know beforehand how to score it. The skeleton of the evidentiary argument, and a way to incorporate particulars, has already been laid out. We will have produced a reusable student model that we can use to project an overall score for licensing but that supports mid-level feedback as well. We will have produced reusable evidence and task models around which DISC can write indefinitely many unique cases, along with a framework for writing case-specific evaluation rules. The technology for scoring, work product evaluation, and simulation can be applied in other products and in other learning domains.

We may conclude by contrasting two approaches for making sense of complex assessment data in ongoing, large-scale applications. The hard way is to ask "How do you score it?" after you have built the assessment and scripted the tasks or scenarios. Unfortunately, the contrasting approach is not "the easy way" but a different hard way: Design the assessment and the tasks or scenarios around what you want to make inferences about, what you need to see to ground those inferences, and the structure of the interrelationships. This still is not easy, but it just might work.

ACKNOWLEDGMENTS

This article was based on research conducted for the Dental Interactive Simulation Corporation (DISC) by the Chauncey Group International, Educational Testing Service, and the DISC Scoring Team: Barry Wohlgemuth, DISC President and Project Director; Lynn Johnson, Project Manager; Gene Kramer; and five core dental hygienist members, Phyllis Beemsterboer, RDH, Cheryl Cameron, RDH, JD, Ann Eshenaur, RDH, Karen Fulton, RDH, and Lynn Ray, RDH. Robert J. Mislevy's work was supported in part by the Educational Research and Development Centers Program, PR/Award R305B60002, as administered by the Office of Educational Research and Improvement, U.S. Department of Education. The findings and opinions expressed in this report do not reflect the positions or policies of the National Institute on Student Achievement, Curriculum, and Assessment, the Office of Educational Research and Improvement, or the U.S. Department of Education.

REFERENCES

Almond, R. G., Herskovits, E., Mislevy, R. J., & Steinberg, L. S. (1999). Transfer of information between system and evidence models. In D. Heckerman & J. Whittaker (Eds.), *Artificial intelligence and statistics 99* (pp. 181–186). San Francisco: Morgan Kaufmann.

Almond, R. G., & Mislevy, R. J. (1999). Graphical models and computerized adaptive testing. *Applied Psychological Measurement, 23*, 223–237.

Bennett, R. E. (1999). Using new technology to improve assessment. *Educational Measurement: Issues and Practice, 18*, 5–12.

Cameron, C. A., Beemsterboer, P. L., Johnson, L. A., Mislevy, R. J., Steinberg, L. S., & Breyer, F. J. (1999). A cognitive task analysis for dental hygiene. *Journal of Dental Education, 64*, 333–351.

Edwards, W. (1998). Hailfinder: Tools for and experiences with Bayesian normative modeling. *American Psychologist, 53*, 416–428.

Ericsson, K. A., & Smith, J., (1991). Prospects and limits of the empirical study of expertise: An introduction. In K. A. Ericsson & J. Smith (Eds.), *Toward a general theory of expertise: Prospects and limits* (pp. 1–38). Cambridge, England: Cambridge University Press.

Gardner, H. (1991). *The unschooled mind: How children think, and how schools should teach.* New York: Basic Books.

Glaser, R., Lesgold, A., & Lajoie, S. (1987). Toward a cognitive theory for the measurement of achievement. In R. Ronning, J. Glover, J. C. Conoley, & J. Witt (Eds.), *The influence of cognitive psychology on testing and measurement: The Buros-Nebraska Symposium on measurement and testing* (Vol. 3, pp. 41–85). Hillsdale, NJ: Lawrence Erlbaum Associates, Inc.

Greeno, J. G., Collins, A. M., & Resnick, L. B. (1997). Cognition and learning. In D. Berliner & R. Calfee (Eds.), *Handbook of educational psychology* (pp. 15–47). New York: Simon & Schuster Macmillan.

Jensen, F. V. (1996). *An introduction to Bayesian networks.* New York: Springer-Verlag.

Johnson, L. A., Wohlgemuth, B., Cameron, C. A., Caughtman, F., Koertge, T., Barna, J., & Schultz, J. (1998). Dental Interactive Simulations Corporation (DISC): Simulations for education, continuing education, and assessment. *Journal of Dental Education, 62*, 919–928.

Kahneman, D., Slovic, P., & Tversky, A. (1982). *Judgment under uncertainty: Heuristics and biases.* Cambridge, England: Cambridge University Press.

Lesgold, A. M., Rubinson, H., Feltovich, P. J., Glaser, R., Klopfer, D., & Wang, Y. (1988). Expertise in a complex skill: Diagnosing X-ray pictures. In M. T. H. Chi, R. Glaser, & M. J. Farr (Eds.), *The nature of expertise* (pp. 311–342). Hillsdale, NJ: Lawrence Erlbaum Associates, Inc.

Melnick, D. (1996). The experience of the National Board of Medical Examiners. In E. L. Mancall, P. G. Vashook, & J. L. Dockery (Eds.), *Computer-based examinations for board certification* (pp. 111–120). Evanston, IL: American Board of Medical Specialties.

Messick, S. (1994). The interplay of evidence and consequences in the validation of performance assessments. *Educational Researcher, 23*(2), 13–23.

Mislevy, R. J. (1994). Evidence and inference in educational assessment. *Psychometrika, 59*, 439–483.

Mislevy, R. J. (1995). Probability-based inference in cognitive diagnosis. In P. Nichols, S. Chipman, & R. Brennan (Eds.), *Cognitively diagnostic assessment* (pp. 43–71). Hillsdale, NJ: Lawrence Erlbaum Associates, Inc.

Mislevy, R. J., Almond, R. G., Yan, D., & Steinberg, L. S. (1999). Bayes nets in educational assessment: Where do the numbers come from? In K. B. Laskey & H. Prade (Eds.), *Proceedings of the Fifteenth Conference on Uncertainty in Artificial Intelligence* (pp. 437–446). San Francisco: Morgan Kaufmann.

Mislevy, R. J., & Gitomer, D. H. (1996). The role of probability-based inference in an intelligent tutoring system. *User-Modeling and User-Adapted Interaction, 5,* 253–282.

Mislevy, R. J., Senturk, D., Almond, R. G., Dibello, L. V., Jenkins, F., Steinberg, L. S., & Yan, D. (in press). *Modeling conditional probabilities in complex educational assessments* (CSE Tech. Rep.). Los Angeles, CA: The National Center for Research on Evaluation, Standards, Student Testing, Center for Studies in Education, University of California, Los Angeles.

Mislevy, R. J., Steinberg, L. S., & Almond, R. G. (2002a). On the several roles of task model variables in assessment design. In S. Irvine & P. Kyllonen (Eds.), *Generating items for cognitive tests: Theory and practice* (pp. 97–128). Mahwah, NJ: Lawrence Erlbaum Associates, Inc.

Mislevy, R. J., Steinberg, L. S., & Almond, R. G. (2002b). On the structure of educational assessments. *Measurement: Interdisciplinary Research and Perspectives, 1,* 3–62.

Misley, R. J., Steinberg, L. S., Breyer, F. J., Almond, R. G., & Johnson, L. A. (1999). A cognitive task analysis, with implications for designing a simulation-based assessment system. *Computers and Human Behavior, 15,* 335–374.

Mislevy, R. J., Wilson, M. R., Ercikan, K., & Chudowsky, N. (in press). Psychometric principles in student assessment. In D. Stufflebeam & T. Kellaghan (Eds.), *International handbook of educational evaluation.* Dordrecht, The Netherlands: Kluwer Academic.

Newell, A., & Simon, H. A. (1972). *Human problem solving.* Englewood Cliffs, NJ: Prentice Hall.

Pellegrino, J., Chudowsky, N., & Glaser, R. (Eds.). (2001). *Knowing what students know: The science and design of educational assessment* (National Research Council's Committee on the Foundations of Assessment). Washington, DC: National Academy Press.

Pennington, N., & Hastie, R. (1991). A cognitive theory of juror decision making: The story model. *Cardozo Law Review, 13,* 519–557.

Schum, D. A. (1994). *The evidential foundations of probabilistic reasoning.* New York: Wiley.

Spiegelhalter, D. J., Thomas, A., Best, N. G., & Gilks, W. R. (1995). *BUGS: Bayesian inference using Gibbs sampling, Version 0.50.* Cambridge, England: MRC Biostatistics Unit.

APPENDIX

A Simple Example Using Bayes Nets in Assessment

This appendix offers a simple example of how Bayes nets can be used in assessment. The interested reader is referred to Mislevy (1994, 1995) and Mislevy and Gitomer (1996) for additional discussion and examples. There is just one student model variable in this small example: Level of Proficiency. It has two levels, expert and novice, and we assume a student is unambiguously one or the other. The work product is the examinee's sequence of actions in taking a patient history in a particular task situation, and we assume we can determine unambiguously whether a given sequence is adequate or inadequate. What we want to do in the assessment setting is observe an examinee's history taking, evaluate its adequacy, and update our belief about the examinee's expert/novice status. The following is a numerical illustration of how one moves from state of relative ignorance about the unknown value of the student model variable to a state of greater knowledge by incorporating value of evidence from an observed variable.

Figure A1 is a matrix of conditional probabilities for taking an adequate or an inadequate patient history in a particular situation, given that the actor is an expert or is a novice. The top row gives conditional probabilities of .8 and .2 for observing an adequate and inadequate history respectively from a participant known to be an expert. We assume for the moment that we know these values cold; we have just run an experiment in which we have observed the history taking of 10,000 acknowledged experts and noted that 8,000 took adequate histories and 2,000 took inadequate ones. Similarly, the bottom row gives conditional probabilities of .4 and .6 for observing an adequate and inadequate history, respectively, to be taken by a novice. Note that this is reasoning from proficiency to expectations for observables, just the opposite of what we want to do in assessment.

Now let's reason in the other direction. We have done our experiments, so we know experts take adequate histories 80% of the time and novices do 40% of the time. If a new examinee with an unknown proficiency takes an adequate history, how should this evidence influence our belief about his or her level of expertise? The "Adequate history = yes" column gives the answer: We should shift our beliefs by a factor of .8/.4, or 2-to-1, toward Expert. Technically, this column is the likelihood that observing an adequate history induces. Analogously, if we observe that an inadequate history has been taken, we should modify our beliefs by a factor of .2/.6, or 1-to-3, shifting toward Novice.

The first panel of Figure A2 shows the probability distributions that express our beliefs *after* the experiment for getting the conditional probabilities but *before* observing the response of the next new examinee. It assumes 50–50 chances that this new examinee is an expert or a novice, as indicated by the bars at .5 for the two possible proficiency values. If she is an expert, the probability is .8 that she will take an adequate history. If she is a novice, the corresponding probability is .4. Averaged over our 50–50 prior for Expert and Novice status, these expectations imply a .6 probability of observing an adequate history.

Adequate History

Proficiency	Yes	No
Expert	.8	.2
Novice	.4	.6

FIGURE A1   Conditional probability matrix.

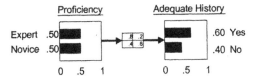

A. Before Observing Response

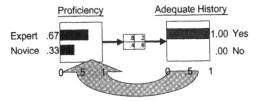

B. After Observing 'Yes' Response

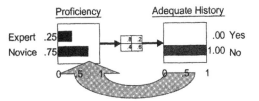

FIGURE A2   Updating beliefs.   C. After Observing 'No' Response

The second panel of Figure A2 shows how our beliefs change if we observe an examinee take an adequate history. The probability for the possible values of "adequate history" is all on "yes" now because we have actually observed it. Our belief that the examinee is an expert has shifted up from 50–50 accordingly, using Bayes theorem to shift the probabilities for expert/novice in the 2-to-1 ratio. The third panel shows how our beliefs change if instead we observe an examinee take an inadequate history. Belief shifts downward, in proportion to the 1-to-3 ratio of conditional probabilities of an inadequate history from an expert and from a novice respectively.

In applied work, for a specific inferential problem, the structure of the Bayes net and the conditional probabilities can often be taken as known. Where do the conditional probabilities come from? Initial estimates of conditional probabilities can come from expert opinion, and they can be refined with pretest data (Mislevy, Almond, Yan, & Steinberg, 1999). This is analogous to estimating item parameters in item response theory. It can be accomplished via Monte Carlo Markov Chain estimation, using, for example, the BUGS computer program (Spiegelhalter, Thomas, Best, & Gilks, 1995).

APPLIED MEASUREMENT IN EDUCATION, *15*(4), 391–412

A Review of Strategies for Validating Computer-Automated Scoring

Yongwei Yang
The Gallup Organization
Lincoln, NE

Chad W. Buckendahl
University of Nebraska–Lincoln

Piotr J. Juszkiewicz and Dennison S. Bhola
The Gallup Organization
Lincoln, NE

Computer-automated scoring (CAS) is becoming a popular tool in assessment. Various studies have been conducted to assess the quality of CAS-system-generated scores. There is then a need for a systematic examination of these studies in the context of contemporary validity concepts and current practice. This article starts with a brief introduction to current CAS systems. Next, we review the current practice of validating CAS-system-generated scores. Finally, we present a conceptual framework and general recommendations for designing validation studies for CAS procedures.

With the advent of new technologies, computer-automated scoring (CAS) systems for scoring constructed-response and performance activities (e.g., essay) are emerging as popular tools in various testing programs. Different CAS procedures have yielded a range of results but, generally, a high level of correspondence between the scores produced by human scorers and CAS systems is reported. Although this evidence of reliability is valuable, questions arise about the validity of the scores generated from these scoring processes. If comparable results are generated using a CAS system, what are the theoretical and empirical implications that arise from using this new technology?

Requests for reprints should be sent to Yongwei Yang, The Gallup Organization, 301 South 68th Street Place, Lincoln, NE 68510. E-mail: yongwei_yang@gallup.com

Although a general framework for a validation design has been offered in the computerized testing arena (Bennett & Bejar, 1998), more systematic examinations of CAS systems in the context of current practice and contemporary validity concepts need to be presented. These examinations will provide a more comprehensive evaluation of the quality of the validity evidence reported in these newer areas of testing. This article presents a conceptual framework for designing validation studies for CAS procedures. We base our core framework largely on the work of Bennett and Bejar (1998) on validating computer-based tests. We expand their framework and present discussions specific to CAS. In addition, we present a review of existing CAS systems and related validation efforts as a context for the discussion of the validation framework.

REVIEW OF CURRENT PRACTICE

Background

Compared to highly structured and objective items, constructed-response items and performance assessments are believed to be more "authentic" in the sense that they present test takers with tasks more similar to those in the actual educational or job settings. These measures may also provide a better understanding of the test takers' thinking processes and, as a result, provide more useful information on subsequent decisions or activities (e.g., instructional intervention, job training, hiring and placement). Inasmuch as constructed-response items and performance assessments make use of more authentic, real-life examples, they are less susceptible to certain test-taking strategies and cheating behaviors (Airasian, 1991).

Despite these advantages, there are also difficulties in incorporating constructed-response items and performance assessments into assessment programs, especially large-scale ones. The most salient obstacles are the high cost, demanding resources, and delayed feedback associated with scoring these items by humans. These financial, human resource, and time constraints limit the number of tasks that can be incorporated in an assessment. As a result, task specificity, a problem that can be largely controlled by adding items when a test consists of objective item types, becomes a serious threat to the reliability and validity of scores with constructed-response items and performance assessments. Furthermore, the financial, human resource, and time constraints limit the types of feedback to a single or a few scores instead of more informative ones for succeeding activities, which in turn largely defeats the advantages of using constructed-response items and performance assessments. Finally, regardless of the high level of expertise and high quality of training, human-generated scores still show a certain degree of instability, both between scorers and within a scorer across time and occasions (Traub, 1994). Such instability introduces an additional source of measurement error.

It was the desire to apply constructed-response and performance assessment and to address the drawbacks from using human scorers that motivated researchers to develop CAS systems. In the field of education, attempts to develop CAS systems date back to the late 1960s when Ellis Page developed the first generation of Project Essay Grader (PEG; Kukich, 2000; Page, 1966, 1994). To date, a number of CAS systems have been used in various assessment programs.

Skepticism and critiques have accompanied CAS systems since their conception. Some of the criticisms concerned logistics issues, such as the cost and time of developing CAS systems and the availability of computers and other technologies required to implement them. Others address more fundamental issues regarding the validity of CAS-system-generated scores, such as the overreliance on surface features of responses, the insensitivity to the content of responses and to creativity, and the vulnerability to new types of cheating and test-taking strategies. However, with the new advances in theories and technologies as well as the increasing accessibility to computers and the Internet, these concerns have been addressed to some level of satisfaction.

In general, two important improvements contribute to the increasing popularity of CAS systems. First, compared to earlier procedures, which relied heavily on surface elements, current CAS systems rely more on the deeper structures of responses that are more relevant to the constructs of interest. Next, these CAS systems have been undergoing increasingly sophisticated evaluations regarding their appropriateness and utility. Improving under such intense scrutiny further increased the popularity and credibility of the CAS systems. It was in the context of these improvements that Williamson, Bejar, and Hone (1999) were able to present eight advantages of using modern CAS systems over human scoring: reproducibility, consistency, tractability, item specification, granularity, objectivity, reliability, and efficiency.

In the following sections we present descriptions of several CAS systems currently operating and attempts at collecting validity evidence. Four of these systems focus on scoring essays, others were designed to score constructed-response items. Although these descriptions are by no means comprehensive, we believe these descriptions present a picture that is representative of the current status in this field. Readers interested in the details of specific CAS systems and validation studies are encouraged to consult the literature listed in the references. Also, in this article we do not attempt to compare the quality and usefulness of these systems. We also do not make recommendations of one of them over another. Rather, the following descriptions provide the context for our discussion of a validation framework in the final section.

Current CAS Systems

Project essay grader.   Among the current CAS systems for essay scoring, PEG (Page, 1966, 1994; Page & Petersen, 1995; Page, Poggio, & Keith, 1997; Shermis, 2001; Shermis, Koch, Page, Keith, & Harrington, 1999; Shermis, Rasmussen, Rajecki, Olson, & Marsiglio, 2001) has the longest history (Kukich, 2000). Earlier generations of PEG only provided a holistic score of an essay; however, recent attempts have been made to provide "trait" (e.g., on organization, style) scores for instructional and diagnostic feedback (Shermis et al., 1999).

The significance of PEG to the development of CAS systems is unquestionable. First, the strategy used by PEG developers to generate scoring is also used with many other systems. In general, the strategy consists of three steps (Page, 1994). PEG developers believed that the constructs of interests in a writing assessment (e.g., general writing skill) are latent and cannot be measured directly. Thus the first logical step of developing a CAS system was to identify a set of measurable *proxy* features that are approximations or correlates of those latent variables. After these proxy features were identified, they applied linear multiple regression to find the optimal combination of these features that best predict the ratings of human experts. Finally, the features and the optimal combination were translated into computer programs to be used to score new essays.

This three-step strategy is common in the development of scoring models with many other CAS systems. That is, the development of these scoring models usually involves identification of the constructs of interests and their measurable features, modeling these features to maximize the correspondence of the CAS-generated results with some external criteria (e.g., expert scores, scoring rubric), and translation of the model characteristics to computer programs. Similar to the efforts of the PEG creators, the development of other CAS systems also involves cross-validating the scoring models and lengthy efforts of fine-tuning the models and the programs. The development of these systems differ, however, in their philosophical foundations, their intended purposes, methods used to identify and extract measurable features, methods used to model scoring processes, and the criteria used in modeling and testing the system.

Another contribution of PEG is that from the very beginning it facilitated an important debate regarding the utility of CAS-generated scoring. One of the key issues is whether a computer-based scoring program can or even should be designed to "understand" the content of the responses. PEG's developers claim that their program does not intend to do so. They make that very clear on the PEG Web site: "PEG does not understand the content of your written product, but rather emulates how raters evaluate work that is similar to yours" (http://134.68.49.185/PEGDEMO/). They further argue that it is very difficult, impractical, and perhaps unnecessary to develop a computer program that would be able to understand content, especially with large-scale assessments (Shermis et al., 1999). Others, as we discuss later, believe it is important and possible for computer programs to capture the essence of the content of responses.

Intelligent essay assessor.   Intelligent essay assessor (IEA) was developed in the late 1990s by a group of researchers including Thomas K. Landauer, Darrell

Laham, Peter W. Foltz, and others. Offered by Knowledge Analysis Technologies (KAT), it is now a commercially available product for scoring essays and providing tutorial feedback (Kukich, 2000; Laham, 2001; Landauer, Laham, & Foltz, 2001). Contrasted to PEG, KAT claims on its Web site that "IEA is the only grading application that focuses on meaning and content rather than surface features, such as spelling, grammar, and lists of words" (http://www.knowledge-technologies.com/presskit/KAT_IEA_brief.pdf).

The most unique feature of IEA is the application of latent semantic analysis (LSA) to measure writing quality more directly. LSA is a technology used to judge the semantic relatedness and similarity among documents (e.g., essays). It achieves this goal through statistical analysis of large body of text in a given knowledge domain and establishing a multidimensional semantic space for words and passages used in this domain. The similarity in meaning of two words or two passages, then, can be estimated by comparing their relative positions in a semantic space (Landauer & Dumais, 1997; Landauer, Foltz, & Laham, 1998).

To generate scoring models for essays, IEA first processes a large body of "background" text in the domain of interest. For example, to assess essays written for an introductory psychology class, IEA first processes textbooks and other materials used in the class to establish a semantic space for this domain. Next, IEA calibrates to "mimic" expert scoring by analyzing the semantic contents (expressed statistically in the semantic space established earlier) of a large number of essays, the quality of which has been judged by human experts. In this sense, IEA "learns" about what qualifies to be a good (as well as not so good and bad) essay to human experts. Finally, IEA compares the semantic contents of the essays it has trained on with the semantic contents of the new essays to be scored. Then, it predicts how the human judges would have scored them (Landauer et al., 2001). In other words, IEA bases its scores "primarily on the opinions of human experts about similar essays, rather than relying on specific key words and other index variables that correlate with human scores on other essays" (Landauer, Laham, & Foltz, 2000, p. 28). Furthermore, IEA is also capable of calibrating based on either model essays from experts, or based on comparisons among a large set of essays themselves (Landauer et al., 2000, 2001).

Intellimetric.   Offered by Vantage Learning, Intellimetric is a CAS system for scoring essays and other essay-type items. Details of the technologies and models it uses are not available. Limited information is provided on its Web site (http://www.intellimetric.com) and by Elliot (2001). According to these sources, Intellimetric incorporates various artificial intelligence techniques and statistical methods. It analyzes 72 features at semantic, syntactic, and discourse levels. These features are grouped into five categories for providing feedback: focus and unity, development and elaboration, organization and structure, sentence structure, and mechanics and conventions. For each essay, prompt, or task to be scored, Intellimetric creates a somewhat unique solution (i.e., scoring model). Different from the common three-step strategy, Intellimetric generates a scoring model by training on a set of prescored responses first, without prespecifying a set of features or rubrics. The system claims to be able to "infer the rubric and the pooled judgments of the human scorers" (Elliot, 2001, p. 2) from these training materials.

E-rater.   Developed in late 1990s by a team of Educational Testing Services (ETS) researchers led by Jill Burstein, e-rater is a CAS system originally designed for scoring essays of the Analytical Writing Assessment section of the Graduate Management Admission Test (Burstein, 2001b; Burstein, Kukich, Wolff, Lu, & Chodorow, 1998; Burstein, Kukich, Wolff, Lu, Chodorow, et al., 1998; Burstein & Marcu, 2000). It is now used as one of the two scorers of the essay portion of the test. The other scorer is a human and when the score discrepancy between the two is more than 1 point (on a scale of 0 to 6), another human scorer is used to settle the difference. Recently, e-rater has also been used by ETS-Technologies, a for-profit subsidiary of ETS, as the core technology of its product called Criterion, a Web-based program for providing immediate scoring and feedback to users about their writing skills. Similar to PEG, e-rater was originally developed to provide a single holistic score but has been improved to be able to generate feedback regarding grammatical and discourse features and errors (Burstein, 2001a). Similar to Intellimetric, e-rater is capable of generating prompt-specific scoring models.

The core technologies of e-rater came from research in the areas of natural language processing (NLP) and information retrieval. These technologies are used to develop three modules, each aimed at identifying one of the three salient characteristics of an essay response: syntactic variety, topic content, and organization of ideas or rhetorical structure (Burstein & Marcu, 2000; Kukich, 2000). Specifically, syntactic variety is analyzed by syntactic-processing tools borrowed from NLP research. Topic content is evaluated by using vector space modeling techniques and vocabulary content analyses. These techniques allow e-rater to assess an essay's content in terms of its similarity with prescored essays at the vocabulary level. Assessment of the rhetorical structure is achieved by partitioning essay into arguments based on lexical syntactic cues and by vocabulary content analysis (Burstein, Kukich, Wolff, Lu, & Chodorow, 1998; Burstein, Kukich, Wolff, Lu, Chodorow, et al., 1998; Kukich, 2000). To generate a scoring model for a specific essay prompt, a scoring rubric needs to be developed to specify writing features of various scoring levels. These features are not only to be used to predict human scores, but also to be meaningful in the context of writing assessment. Next, e-rater processes a set of training essays prescored by expert raters. It identifies relevant features through both deriving them statistically and extracting them with NLP techniques. It then uses stepwise linear regression technique to find the optimal combinations of these features that best predicts expert ratings. Finally, the resulting model is used to create the scoring program for an essay.

E-rater was designed to score essay-type responses—responses that are not too short. On its Web site (http://www.etstechnologies.com/scoringtech-crater.htm), ETS Technologies claims it is also developing a new product, called c-rater or concept-rater, for scoring short-answer constructed-responses.

CAS system for assessing physicians' patient management skills.   The preceding four systems are applications for scoring essays designed to measure writing skills. There are also applications of CAS systems to score other types of constructed-response items. The system developed by Stephen Clyman and his colleagues for the National Board of Medical Examiners is one such application. This system was designed for scoring computer-simulated performance assessment of physicians' patient management skills (Clauser, Harik, & Clyman, 2000; Clauser, Margolis, Clyman, & Ross, 1997; Clauser, Ross, et al., 1997; Clauser et al., 1995; Clauser, Swanson, & Clyman, 1999). In this assessment, examinees are presented with a simulated patient care environment. The simulated situation advances in a virtual timeline and examinees are asked to type in text entries of activities such as order specific tests, treatments, and so on. The final response is a transaction list consisting of entries given by an examinee (Clauser et al., 1995).

To develop an optimal CAS system, Clyman and his colleagues experimented with two different strategies. One of them was regression based and the other one was rule based. With the regression-based approach, a committee of clinicians was first asked to develop a detailed scoring rubric. Each feature defined in the scoring rubric was quantifiable by simply counting its presence or absence in a transaction list. Next, these features were used in the linear regression-based scoring model in which the criterion variable was the rating based on consensus of experts. The modeling process involved generating a weighted combination of the features that best predict experts' ratings (Clauser et al., 1995; Clauser, Margolis, et al., 1997). The rule-based approach also started with expert judgment. In this situation, a committee of experts was asked to articulate features that describe the performance associated with each score level. These rules were then operationalized by defining and describing specific combinations of desirable and undesirable examinee actions. Last, these combinations of actions were translated into logical arguments in computer scoring algorithms. Essentially, this approach attempted to use complex rules to map a specific performance with a score level (Clauser, Margolis, et al., 1997; Clauser, Ross, et al., 1997). In several studies (e.g., Clauser, Margolis, et al., 1997; Clauser, Ross, et al., 1997), the regression-based approach consistently performed slightly better than did the rule-based approach.

CAS system used in the architect registration examination.   Developed by Isaac Bejar and his associates in the early 1990s, this system aims at scoring the architectural site-design problems from the graphic simulation divisions of the Architect Registration Examination by the National Council of Architectural Registration Boards. These graphic simulation divisions are made up of a series of vignettes. Each of these vignettes has a description of requirements and a basic design diagram. The examinees then modify the diagram on computer to meet the requirements specified. Williamson, Bejar, and Hone (1999) referred to the development strategy of their system as a "mental model" approach. The term *mental model* is used to "emphasize the effort involved in incorporating not only criteria but also the uncertainty evaluations, judgment, and aggregation processes of experts into the automated scoring, thus capturing the complete mental model experts utilize in desirable scoring process" (Williamson, Bejar, & Hone, 1999, p. 163). In short, their approach also started with the expert committee establishing scoring criteria. Experts were asked to describe characteristics of typical solutions at each score level. Quantifiable features are derived from these descriptions and are used to calibrate a set of scoring rules, using expert rating as criterion. The calibration of scoring rules used both statistical and inductive analyses. The resulting rules, then, did not take on a regression-type equation. Rather, they took on a form of a series of logical functions (Bejar, 1991; Bejar & Braun, 1994; Williamson, Bejar, & Hone, 1999).

CAS system being developed for dentistry assessments.   In the 1990s, the Dental Interactive Simulation Corporation (DISC) began developing computerized assessments that simulate the work of practicing professionals in dentistry (Johnson et al., 1998). The nature of the assessments seeks to provide evidence of the cognitive processes that dental hygienists go through as they perform their jobs. Measuring these processes may link the assessments currently part of the dental profession, namely selected response examinations that measure content knowledge, with clinical assessments that measure the skills needed to perform procedures (Mislevy, Steinberg, Breyer, Almond, & Johnson, 2002).

In the development of the DISC assessments, Mislevy et al. (2002) used a cognitive psychological approach to define levels of performance among candidates (e.g., expert, competent, novice). Measuring these cognitive processes will inform prelicensure and continuing education efforts as curriculum and instruction are modified to target the requisite skills. The DISC simulator constructs the assessment based on what Mislevy et al. (2002) called the conceptual assessment framework. This framework provides an evidentiary basis for the tasks and processes in the assessment (see Johnson et al., 1998, for comprehensive description of the simulator).

The scoring process for the DISC simulation assessments is based on a combination of judgmental decision rules articulated by content experts through predefined skills and abilities and by statistical modeling that incorporates Bayesian characteristics (Mislevy et al., 2002). The elements of the scoring process are integrated to determine a level of predefined proficiency that may provide meaningful feedback to candidates seeking licensure but also give the training programs information about how to adapt their curriculum and inform instruction.

Other CAS systems for scoring constructed-responses. There are yet other CAS systems that have been developed and tested for scoring constructed-response items. For example, Braun, Bennett, Frye, and Soloway (1990) described the applications of expert systems for scoring and diagnosing responses to a type of items on the College Board's Advanced Placement Computer Science exam. This "constrained constructed-response" (Braun et al., 1990) type of items presents examinees with a faulty solution to a computer programming task and asks them to correct it. Two expert systems, PROUST and MicroPROUST, were originally designed to detect certain types of bugs in Pascal programs. In Braun et al. (1990), these two systems were investigated in terms of their ability to provide diagnostic comments and scores. The results showed improvement in performance when the two systems were used to analyze the constrained constructed-responses, compared to the results from analyzing unconstrained responses. In another study, Bennett and Sebrechts (1996) investigated the utility of using an expert system named GIDE Algebra (Sebrechts, 1992) to provide grades and descriptions of errors for mathematics items.

Summary. The intended purposes of the CAS systems we discussed ranged from assessing writing skills, to computer programming, to physician skills; from providing scores to providing descriptive feedback. The item types ranged from constrained constructed-responses to highly free responses. The technologies used by these systems consist of applications of a blend of theories and methods from artificial intelligence, statistical modeling, and cognitive psychology. It is noteworthy that there seems to be two general strategies leading to the development of CAS systems. One is based on empirically derived statistical relationships, and the other is based on rules, mental models, principles, or policies believed to be used by human scorers. There is also a tendency to integrate the two approaches to optimize outcomes.

Current Validation Practice

Naturally, with the proliferation of CAS systems, there is a growing body of literature on the attempts made to validate the meaning and uses of CAS-system-generated scores. Various approaches have been used in these validation studies. In this section, we summarize these approaches rather than their results. We believe these approaches may be classified into three general types. The first approach focuses on the relationship among scores given to the same instrument by different scorers. The second approach focuses on the relationship between these scores and external measures. The third approach focuses on the scoring processes and the mental models represented by the CAS systems. We discuss these three approaches separately.

Relationships among scores generated by different scorers.   Because constructed-responses and performance assessments may be initially scored by human scorers, a straightforward way to demonstrate the accuracy and appropriateness of CAS-system-generated scores is to evaluate their relationship to the scores assigned by human scorers to the same item (e.g., task, prompt) or the same test. The simplest way to demonstrate the correspondence is by showing that scores given by CAS systems have a high *level of agreement* with those given by trained scorers. Various methods exist for assessing the level of agreement. When the scoring scale is discrete and consists of a small number of points, a popular index is the percentage of agreement between two scoring methods (e.g., Burstein, Kukich, Wolff, Lu, & Chodorow, 1998). It is computed by dividing the number of instances in which two methods assigned the same score by the total number of instances. This is sometimes called *percent of exact agreement*. With items utilizing a reasonable multiple-points scoring scale, one can also compute the percent of adjacent agreement. In this case, the numerator is the number of instances in which two methods agreed within 1 point difference (i.e., either exact agreement or the score difference is 1 point). Furthermore, one can also compare the agreement between two human experts and between a CAS system and a human expert to demonstrate that a CAS system is no less consistent than human experts (Burstein, Kukich, Wolff, Lu, & Chodorow, 1998; Elliot, 2001).

Although the computation of percent of agreement is straightforward and the results are easy to communicate with lay audiences, the method is problematic. This index can be misleading because it is also sensitive to the number of score points, the total number of instances studied, and the marginal distributions of scores. To address some of these issues, researchers have also used other rater agreement indices, such as Cohen's Kappa (e.g., Bejar, 1991; Burstein, Marcu, Andreyev, & Chodorow, 2001; Clauser, Ross, et al., 1997; Williamson et al., 1999), which adjusts for chance agreement. Furthermore, there are other means to address the correspondence between scores generated by CAS systems and human scorers. One way is to compare the distributions of scores generated from different methods (Elliot, 2001). Another way is to compute a correlation between scores. With this method, one can investigate the reliability of CAS-system-generated scores by correlating them with expert scores as well as by comparing the reliability of scores assigned by human scorers and by a CAS system (e.g., Burstein, Kukich, Wolff, Lu, & Chodorow, 1998; Clauser, Margolis, et al., 1997; Clauser, Ross, et al., 1997; Landauer et al., 2000; Page, 1966, 1994; Page & Petersen, 1995; Page et al., 1997; Shermis et al., 1999).

The methods described here evaluate the correspondence between observed scores. Researchers have also attempted to assess the correspondence between CAS-system-generated scores and expert scores at the true score level. With subjectively scored items, one way to conceptualize a true score is to treat it as the expected score assigned by human scorers, which can be estimated by averaging the scores from a large number of experts. For example, validation studies for PEG used average ratings from two to eight judges as the estimate of essay's true score (Page, 1994; Page & Petersen, 1995; Page et al., 1997; Shermis et al., 1999). It is also possible to approximate the true scores by using the consensus scores given by a group of experts (e.g., in Clauser et al., 1995). These consensus scores are not the mathematical averages of individual expert scores. They are the scores a group of experts agreed on after discussions. It is important to point out that the estimation of true score correlation is a somewhat complicated issue and different methods should be used for different situations (e.g., see the appendix in Clauser et al., 1999). In addition to using correlation, some researchers also used confirmatory factor analysis to show the relationship between CAS-system-assigned scores and true scores (Shermis et al., 1999).

In the published literature, both agreement/reliability approaches and true score approaches demonstrate desirable performance of CAS systems across various domains and populations. However, it is useful to point out the different implications between these two approaches. With the former, where CAS-system-generated scores are compared with scores assigned by a single rater, a perfect agreement or correlation may not be desirable. This is because theoretically the agreement between scores given by human scorers cannot be perfect in the long run—there are always variations due to intrarater inconsistency and interrater differences. If a CAS system produces scores that agree completely with a human rater, it may indicate that the system not only modeled the construct-relevant aspects of a scoring process but also possibly emulated the personal and situational characteristics that may contribute to the errors and biases in measurement. Under the same logic, it is possible for scores produced by a CAS system to correlate higher with scores from an expert than scores produced by another expert. This is because a CAS system can generate scores that are more consistent due to the mechanical nature of its scoring processes (Clauser et al., 2000; Landauer et al., 2000). With true score approaches, on the other hand, it is desirable to have perfect true score correlation. This is because such a correlation indicates the true scores obtained from two methods (i.e., CAS system and experts) are equivalent or related through a linear transformation.

Preceding approaches are all based on classical test theory's conceptualization of true score and reliability. Researchers have also applied generalizability theory to evaluate the measurement precision of scores produced by CAS systems as well as to compare the precision between scores generated by CAS systems and human experts (Clauser et al., 2000; Clauser et al., 1999). After establishing the correspondence between the true scores, these generalizability theory studies also tended to demonstrate that the CAS system performed at least as well as human experts.

Relationship between test score and external measures.   Approaches focusing on the relationship among scores given to the same instrument by different scorers are used by researchers to address the issues of consistency and precision of CAS-system-generated scores. The relationship between these scores and other variables, on the other hand, are used to address broader validity questions. Some studies evaluated the relationship between the CAS-system-generated scores with other measures of the same or similar constructs of interest (Elliot, 2001; Shermis et al., 1999). Landauer et al. (2001) investigated the differential agreement between IEA scores and rating given by people with different levels of domain expertise. They showed that the IEA-generated scores agreed better with ratings given by people with higher rather than lower expertise.

When responses to a task can be seen as either pass or fail, one can also evaluate the quality of CAS-system-generated scores by investigating the consistency between decisions based on these scores and those given by experts. Clauser and his associates used this approach to evaluate the quality of the scores given by their CAS system for physicians' patient management skills (Clauser, Ross, et al., 1997; Clauser et al., 1995). To do so, they asked experts to assign pass–fail categories to a set of transaction lists that were scored independently in four different ways: by another group of experts and by three different CAS systems. They then compared the score distributions of the pass and fail groups with each of the four scoring methods. The results showed that their regression-based CAS system performed as well as expert scorers (and better than other methods) in terms of effectively separating the pass–fail groups.

Approaches focusing on scoring processes.   In addition to the validation efforts based on demonstrating statistical relationships between scores, many researchers have also stressed the importance of understanding the scoring processes that CAS systems used. As Landauer et al. (2000) put it, there is a need to "make sure that the factor that the machine is measuring … is one we want to stress" (p. 29). This might be counterintuitive because one may think that CAS systems are developed by experts who know how a response *should be* scored. However, as noted previously, the development of scoring models in many of the CAS systems relied to some extent on statistical methods to identify scoring features and combinations of these features that best *predict* human scores. These data-driven statistical procedures that aimed to maximize predictive accuracy do not address the meaningfulness of the features they selected. Rather, such meaningfulness can only be addressed with additional empirical and theoretical investigations.

There are ways to address this issue with correlational or experimental studies. For example, Landauer and his colleagues compared the relative contributions of different components in the IEA scoring model in terms of predicting expert scores. They showed that the component that had the largest contribution was the one related to the content of the responses (Laham, 2001; Landauer et al., 2001).

It is also necessary to use approaches descriptive and qualitative in nature to evaluate the scoring processes of CAS systems. For example, by analyzing the patterns and nature of disagreement between expert ratings and CAS-system-generated scores, one may identify the differences between human and computer scoring models in terms of the factors considered and the relative weighting of these factors (Burstein, Kukich, Wolff, Lu, & Chodorow, 1998; Clauser, Margolis, et al., 1997; Williamson et al., 1999). Aimed at improving the performance of e-rater, Powers, Burstein, Chodorow, Fowles, and Kukich (2001) invited experts to "trick the system." They found experts were more successful in misleading e-rater to overrate an essay rather than to underrate it. By analyzing the patterns of these results as well as the strategies used by experts to trick the computer program, they were able to show that e-rater and experts may treat some meaningful features differently when grading essays. Based on these results, improvements could be made to both the computer program and the human grading rubrics.

Summary.   In this section, we discussed various methods that have been used to validate the meaning and uses of CAS-system-generated scores. Among them, there are quantitative and qualitative approaches. The quantitative methods include descriptive statistics, correlational studies, and statistical modeling that look at agreement levels, reliability analyses, or generalizability theory applications. We have also seen the differential emphasis on certain methods in relation to the differences in development strategies of CAS systems and in the intended use of scores. In general, to the extent that a CAS system is used to provide scores rather than instructional or diagnostic feedback, validation efforts focused more on applying statistical methods to demonstrate correspondence between scorers than on the nature and processes of the scoring models used by computer. In addition, to the extent that the development of a CAS system is based on aligning its scoring models with those used by experts rather than on statistical modeling with empirical data, more emphasis was put on qualitative analysis than the meaning of scores given by computer. The questions, then, are

1. Will the evidence gathered through these methods sufficiently establish the validity of CAS-system-generated scores?
2. What is the appropriate and important validity evidence for CAS-system-generated scores in different situations?

In the next section, we discuss these two questions in the context of contemporary validity concepts in general and specific issues related to using CAS systems.

VALIDATION OF CAS-SYSTEM-GENERATED SCORES

Overview of Modern Validity Concepts

Validity is arguably the most important concept of psychological and educational measurement. Originally defined as the degree to which the test measures what it purports to measure, the meaning of validity has changed substantially over the last 60 years (Anastasi, 1986; Angoff, 1988; Cronbach, 1971, 1988; Embretson, 1983; Geisinger, 1992; Kane, 1992; Kane, Crooks, & Cohen, 1999; Messick, 1988, 1989, 1995). Today validity is viewed as the degree to which both theory and empirical evidence support the inferences and actions based on test scores. Validation, then, is an ongoing process of developing a sound scientific argument and gathering evidence that supports the intended interpretation and actions based on the test scores and that refutes plausible alternative interpretations. This view of validity and validation has been incorporated in the latest Standards for Educational and Psychological Testing (American Educational Research Association, 1999).

There are key characteristics to the contemporary view of validity. Instead of being a property of a test, validity is now considered a property of the inferences based on scores from a test. Therefore, to pursue a line of inquiry designed to validate inferences based on test scores, a clear statement of the intended use and inferences of the test scores must be presented. Once the intended inferences are articulated, the process of gathering evidence can be planned to lend credence to these inferences.

Validation evidence may be derived from empirical data, expert judgments, relevant literature, and logical analysis. Traditionally, the evidence was categorized into content, criterion-related, and construct validity. With the contemporary view of validity, these various types of evidence are gathered to demonstrate the representativeness and relevance of the test scores to the construct intended to be measured. Contemporary validity theory also stresses the consideration of consequences of the interpretation and uses of test scores. That is, test validation should also include the evaluation of the values implied from score interpretations, as well as of the social consequences from using the test. Emphasizing the consequences of test interpretation and uses expands the domain of test validation efforts. As Geisinger (1992) put it, "validation may be best thought of as the evaluation of a test much as program evaluation is the evaluation of a delivery system" (p. 210).

Revisiting Current Validation Efforts of CAS-Generated Scores

How much, then, are the validation efforts made to CAS-generated scores consistent with the contemporary validity theory? First, many of these published validation studies, especially the more recent ones, did include discussions on the purpose of the test for which a CAS system was developed, both in terms of the supposed meaning of the test scores and the intended uses of them. Second, the validation studies consisted of a wide variety of evidence, including those regarding the measurement precision of scores, the meaning of the scores, the scoring processes of CAS systems, and the relationships with external variables. By providing a wide variety of evidence, researchers were trying to present a complete picture of the appropriateness of using CAS systems to generate test scores. In short, these efforts implied an awareness of the importance of the relationship between test purpose and test validation processes. They also demonstrated an understanding of the complexity of validity evidence.

These efforts, however, do have limitations. For the most part, these limitations are not about the soundness of specific methods used; rather, they relate to two issues. First, there is a lack of research on the potential threats to construct relevancy pertaining to the use of CAS systems. Incorporating a CAS system usually implies that a testing program is to some extent computer based, either just its scoring process or, more often, the test delivery and the reporting of results. On the other hand there is a wealth of knowledge regarding the potential construct irrelevant variance that is associated with computer-based testing. For example, the Guidelines for Computer-Based Testing (Association of Test Publishers, 2002) listed specific threats of this type, such as test takers' anxiety about the computer-testing mode, their lack of familiarity with the computer interface in general, or some specific operations needed to complete the computer-based tasks. Research that connects these issues with validating CAS-system-generated scores is rarely seen.

Second, put under the broader concept of validity, this issue implies a lack of research on the consequential evidence in the validation of scores generated by CAS system. In addition to the potential threats to construct relevancy of the test scores, the consequences of incorporating a CAS system may be also evaluated in terms of its influence on the entire testing program and the subsequent social impact. Some researchers did attempt to address these issues. For example, Landauer et al. (2000) stressed the importance of making sure "that the factor the machine is measuring better is one we want to stress" so that the use of the resulting scores do not mislead students to "focus on the wrong things" (p. 29). Many researchers also often start their articles or presentations with a conceptual discussion regarding the potential benefit that CAS system could bring in terms of reducing test cost and increasing the use of authentic assessment. Nevertheless, research beyond this type of conceptual discussion is not common practice yet.

We understand that these limitations may be partly due to the relatively short history of the applications of CAS as well as to the fact that most of the systems were developed to be an alternative or substitute of human scorers. It is then understandable that most of the efforts are made to demonstrate the immediate positive outcomes of using CAS systems, such as showing the correspondence between computer- and human-generated scores. Also, many of the consequential issues just raised cannot be addressed in a short time. Nevertheless, we propose it is important to encourage a sophisticated and complete view of validity. Such a view would facilitate a balance between validation efforts emphasizing test interpretation and test use as well as between investigating intended and unintended consequences. For these reasons, we believe a conceptual framework to guide the efforts of validating CAS-system-generated scores is needed. Such a framework should reflect contemporary validity theory and address the specific issues raised by using CAS systems. We outline such a framework next.

Toward a Validation Framework

Bennett and Bejar's (1998) article represents an original and successful attempt to present a framework for validating computer-based test scores. Much in line with contemporary validity theory, they argued that the scoring method should be considered as a dynamic component of a larger computer-based testing system. Such a testing system consists of several interrelated components. In addition to the scoring module, there are test development tools, examinee interface, tutorials, and reporting methods. Some of these components relate to each other directly. More important, they all relate through the definition of testing constructs and the design of test content.

The interrelatedness among these components is obvious because decisions made on one of them would eventually directly or indirectly affect the others. Because the emphasis of the article is on CAS systems, we focus on the relationships of which the scoring method is a part. First, the definition of the constructs a test intends to measure as well as the intended inferences and uses of scores strongly influence the decision on what, if any, type of CAS system should be considered. If open-ended item types are necessary and using a large number of human scorers is not practical, then a CAS system will be tremendously beneficial to such a testing program. If the test is to be used to provide instructional feedback, then incorporating some rule-based and content-oriented strategies may be preferable to statistical modeling to develop a CAS system to promote wider acceptance among users and consumers.

In terms of test design and the interface for examinees, more naturalistic item types and less constrained test interface almost always require a more sophisticated scoring system. In this situation, the scoring system needs to be able to disentangle relevant and irrelevant behaviors. Failing to do so would subject the resulting scores to the threat of construct irrelevant variance. On the other hand, less complex scoring rubrics, though easy to program, require the item type and testing interface to be more restrictive. However, these easy-to-score items may measure somewhat different constructs from those measured by open-ended ones and may provide limited information for diagnosis and instruction. If the use of a CAS system requires changes to the stimulus presented on a test, and if this in turn causes dramatic changes in the construct measured, then the precision or consistency of the scoring process does not matter—test scores in this case may be consistently measuring something different from the target construct. This reduces the confidence in the inferences made on performance.

There are legitimate concerns regarding the potential threats to validity of testing with the use of CAS systems; the constraints set by the testing constructs and testing interface strongly influence what type of CAS system could be of greatest benefit to the testing program. More important, Bennett and Bejar (1998) argued, and we agree, that using CAS systems have the potential to greatly improve the quality of measurement. The development of a sound CAS system necessarily requires a full understanding of the constructs targeted by the test as well as the human response and scoring processes. It requires a higher level of scrutiny on the entire testing program and forces the articulation of issues that might otherwise go unnoticed. These, in turn, would contribute to the clarity of construct definition and better design of the testing procedures, all of which would enhance the validity evidence.

It is also difficult to overlook the social consequences of incorporating CAS systems. These systems have the potential to open the door to wider application of authentic assessment by reducing the cost and time associated with testing. These improved assessments will eventually provide better value to test users and test takers. In the education field, this could lead to a closer connection between assessment and effective instruction with a manageable cost. In the business world, this could mean more cost-effective measurement tools for sourcing, recruiting, selecting, developing, and managing a workforce.

Bennett and Bejar's (1998) emphasis on the interrelatedness among components of a testing system as well as its implication to validation practice provided a foundation of a validation framework for CAS-system-generated scores. In this framework, scoring method is considered as an active part of the system of a testing program. Decisions made on other parts of the system can constrain the appropriate type of scoring method used. On the other hand, decisions made on scoring method would influence other components as well. Furthermore, changes within the system of a testing program would affect its utility and defensibility in larger contexts. With this understanding of the interrelatedness between the scoring method with other aspects of testing, both within and outside a testing program, it is natural to see the interrelatedness among different kinds of validation evidence. As Bennett and Bejar put it, "evaluation of the scoring mechanism in isolation from the rest of the system can constitute only a piece of the larger validation argument" (p. 15). Evidence of agreement between computer-generated and human-generated scores and relationships between test scores and other measures are both needed, just as evidence pertaining to the meaning of the CAS-system-generated scores and the consequences of using a CAS system are also needed. Moreover, all of these pieces of validity evidence should be brought together and interpreted as a whole.

In addition, we argue that one should also evaluate the relative importance and appropriateness of certain validation evidence by considering the level of integration of a CAS system to the entire testing program. Differences in the level of integration reflect the differences in the perceptions of the utility and implications stemming from the use of a CAS system. On one end is the perception of a CAS system as merely a replacement or substitute for human scorers. In other words, the use of CAS system does not change the existing testing format, test delivery medium, and the type of results reported to test takers. In this situation, validation evidence for the human-generated scores can be used as the basis of validating scores generated through the CAS procedures. When compelling validity evidence for human-generated scores has been established, the most important validity evidence of CAS-system-generated scores is their correspondence to human-generated scores. It is important to emphasize that when assessing agreement and reliability of CAS-system-produced scores, multiple indices should be used whenever appropriate. This is because different agreement indices provide related yet different information on the quality of a CAS procedure. In addition, one should present a discussion of the adequacy and relevance of different indices to a given situation.

Furthermore, even in this situation, the fact that a CAS system is used needs to be communicated to test users and test takers. Then, one should address the effect of this knowledge on test users (e.g., whether they will have higher or lower confidence in the scores or whether they will use the scores differently). One should also investigate the effect on the test takers, such as their self-confidence, test anxiety, and test-taking strategies. Finally, one should examine the effect of this knowledge on the general public, such as whether the test or testing program is becoming more or less credible.

We agree with Clauser, Margolis, et al.'s (1997) contention that CAS "is likely to be a requirement if performance assessments are to be implemented in large-scale testing contexts where the level of expertise required of the judges precludes individual expert review of each performance" (p. 157). We further suggest that most testing programs in the future, by design, will likely include a CAS procedure. In these situations, a CAS system will be actively incorporated into a testing program thereby changing the test from inside out. Done correctly, this high level of integration will facilitate long-term and large-scale positive consequences. Under such circumstances, the correspondence between CAS-system-generated and human-generated scores will not constitute the most important validity evidence. It will only be meaningful in the context of other validation evidence collected with the CAS-system-generated scores. In this context, we present following general recommendations. These recommendations are aimed at contributing to the implementation of sound validation studies and at helping the consumers be better able to scrutinize tests.

1. A comprehensive validation plan should be created early in the process. In this validation plan, there should be a defensible and clearly articulated rationale on the decision to incorporate a CAS system into the testing program. Such a plan should also address the effects that a CAS system might have on the various components of the testing program.

2. There should be a description of how the CAS system is integrated into the testing program. There should be predictions, and subsequent evaluations, on the possible consequences and implications of using CAS systems.

3. As noted earlier, the choices made among the various strategies (e.g., rule based, regression based) implemented when developing a CAS system are driven by the intended purposes of testing. Thus, in the context of the intended use of and inferences made on the basis of test scores, one should provide a logically defensible rationale and evidence regarding why and how certain CAS procedures are chosen over others. In addition, cost-benefit analyses are also important in making choices.

4. Furthermore, as Williamson et al. (1999) pointed out, differences in the development strategies also tend to imply different emphasis on various types of validity evidence. As a result, it is necessary to present arguments regarding the relative importance of different validation evidence with respect to the strategies used in developing a CAS system.

5. In any case, multiple approaches should be used to collect validity evidence. The evidence should be collected across reasonably diverse contexts and with reasonably diverse test-taker samples.

6. Like in the situation of low level of integration, multiple indices should be used assessing agreement and reliability of CAS system produced scores and a discussion of the adequacy and relevance of different indices should be presented.

7. With the study of measurement precision, we also encourage the application of generalizability theory whenever it is appropriate. Generalizability theory studies address the sources as well as the sizes of measurement errors. Such information would be useful to optimize test designs and testing procedures. Thus it would be possible to maximize measurement precision given the available resources and other logistic constraints.

8. To date much of the research on CAS systems (e.g., those demonstrate high agreement between computer-generated and human-generated scores) has been conducted on assessments in narrow content areas (e.g., writing skills). We anticipate a growing interest in expanding CAS applications to other areas like personality and affective measurement. However, the generalization of results obtained from one content domain to another needs to be considered with great care.

As the measurement community continues to create innovative technological solutions CAS systems will become more widely used and the need for appropriate validation will become even more critical. This article adds to the conversation regarding validity and validation by presenting a conceptual framework and general recommendations for designing appropriate studies when CAS systems are part of a testing program.

ACKNOWLEDGMENT

An earlier version of this article was presented at the annual meeting of the Midwestern Educational Research Association, October 2001, Chicago.

REFERENCES

American Educational Research Association, American Psychological Association, and National Council on Measurement in Education. (1999). *Standards for educational and psychological testing.* Washington, DC: Author.

Airasian, P. W. (1991). *Classroom assessment.* McGraw-Hill.

Anastasi, A. (1986). Evolving concepts of test validation. *Annual Review of Psychology, 37,* 1–15.

Angoff, W. H. (1988). Validity: An evolving concept. In H. Wainer & H. Braun (Eds.), *Test validity* (pp. 19–32). Hillsdale, NJ: Lawrence Erlbaum Associates, Inc.

Association of Test Publishers. (2002). *Guidelines for computer-based testing.* Washington, DC: Author.

[Draft]. Retrieved DATE from http://www.testpublishers.org/MembersOnly/Members/computer_testing.htm

Bejar, I. I. (1991). A methodology for scoring open-ended architectural design problems. *Journal of Applied Psychology, 76,* 522–532.

Bejar, I. I., & Braun, H. I. (1994). On the synergy between assessment and instruction: Early lessons from computer-based simulations. *Machine-Mediated Learning, 4,* 5–25.

Bennett, R. E., & Bejar, I. I. (1998, Winter). Validity and automated scoring: It's not only the scoring. *Educational Measurement: Issues and Practice,* 9–17.

Bennett, R. E., & Sebrechts, M. M. (1996). The accuracy of expert-system diagnoses of mathematical problem solutions. *Applied Measurement in Education, 9,* 133–150.

Braun, H. I., Bennett, R. E., Frye, D., & Soloway, E. (1990). Scoring constructed responses using expert system. *Journal of Educational Measurement, 27,* 93–108.

Burstein, J. C. (2001a, February). *Automated essay evaluation in criterion.* Paper presented at the Association of Test Publishers Computer-Based Testing: Emerging Technologies and Opportunities for Diverse Applications conference, Tucson, AZ.

Burstein, J. C. (2001b, April). *Automated essay evaluation with natural language processing.* Paper presented at the annual meeting of the National Council of Measurement in Education, Seattle, WA.

Burstein, J. C., Kukich, K., Wolff, S., Lu, C., & Chodorow, M. (1998, April). *Computer analysis of essays.* Paper presented at the annual meeting of the National Council of Measurement in Education, San Diego, CA. Retrieved May 6, 2002, from http://www.ets.org/research/dload/ncmefinal.pdf

Burstein, J. C., Kukich, K., Wolff, S., Lu, C., Chodorow, M., Braden-Harder, L., & Harris, M. D. (1998, August). Automated scoring using a hybrid feature identification technique. In *Proceedings of the 36th annual meeting of the Association of Computational Linguistics* and *17th International Conference on Computational Linguistics* (pp. 206–210). San Francisco: Morgan Kaufman Publishers. Retrieved May 6, 2002, from http://www.ets.org/research/dload/aclfinal.pdf

Burstein, J. C., & Marcu, D. (2000, August). *Benefits of modularity in an automated essay scoring system.* Paper presented at the Workshop on Using Toolsets and Architectures to Build NLP Systems at the 18th International Conference on Computational Linguistics, Luxembourg. Retrieved May 6, 2002, from http://www.ets.org/research/dload/colinga4.pdf

Burstein, J. C., Marcu, D., Andreyev, S., & Chodorow, M. (2001, July). Towards automatic classification of discourse elements in essays. In *Proceedings of the 39th annual meeting of the Association for Computational Linguistics and 10th Conference of the European Chapter of the Association for Computational Computational Linguistics* (pp. 90–97). San Francisco: Morgan Kaufman Publishers. Retrieved May 6, 2002, from http://www.ets.org/research/dload/burstein.pdf

Clauser, B. E., Harik, P., & Clyman, S. G. (2000). The generalizability of scores for a performance assessment scored with a computer-automated scoring system. *Journal of Educational Measurement, 37,* 245–261.

Clauser, B. E., Margolis, M. J., Clyman, S. G., & Ross, L. P. (1997). Development of automated scoring algorithms for complex performance assessments: A comparison of two approaches. *Journal of Educational Measurement, 34,* 141–161.

Clauser, B. E., Ross, L. P., Clyman, S. G., Rose, K. M., Margolis, M. J., Nungester, R. J., et al. (1997). Development of a scoring algorithm to replace expert rating for scoring a complex performance-based assessment. *Applied Measurement in Education, 10,* 345–358.

Clauser, B. E., Subhiyah, R. G., Nungester, R. J., Ripkey, D. R., Clyman, S. G., & McKinley, D. (1995). Scoring a performance-based assessment by modeling the judgments of experts. *Journal of Educational Measurement, 32,* 397–415.

Clauser, B. E., Swanson, D. B., & Clyman, S. G. (1999). A comparison of the generalizability of scores produced by expert raters and automated scoring systems. *Applied Measurement in Education, 12,* 281–299.

Cronbach, L. J. (1971). Test validation. In R. L. Thorndike (Ed.), *Educational measurement* (2nd ed., pp. 443–507). Washington, DC: American Council on Education.

Cronbach, L. J. (1988). Five perspectives on validity argument. In H. Wainer & H. Braun (Eds.), *Test validity* (pp. 3–17). Hillsdale, NJ: Lawrence Erlbaum Associates, Inc.

Elliot, S. M. (2001, April). *IntelliMetric: From here to validity.* Paper presented at the annual meeting of the American Educational Research Association, Seattle, WA.

Embretson, S. E. (1983). Construct validity: Construct representation versus nomothetic span. *Psychological Bulletin, 93,* 179–197.

Geisinger, K. F. (1992). The metamorphosis of test validation. *Educational Psychologist, 27,* 197–222.

Johnson, L. A., Wohlgemuth, B., Cameron, C. A., Caughtman, F., Koertge, T., Barna, J., et al. (1998). Dental Interactive Simulations Corporation (DISC): Simulations for education, continuing education, and assessment. *Journal of Dental Education, 62,* 919–928.

Kane, M. (1992). An argument-based approach to validation. *Psychological Bulletin, 112,* 527–535.

Kane, M., Crooks, T., & Cohen, A. (1999). Validating measures of performance. *Educational Measurement: Issues and Practices, 18*(2), 5–17.

Kukich, K. (2000). Beyond automated essay scoring. *IEEE Intelligent Systems, 15*(5), 22–27. Retrieved May 6, 2002, from http://www.computer.org/intelligent/ex2000/pdf/x5022.pdf

Laham, D. (2001, April). *Automated scoring and annotation of essays with the Intelligent Essay Assessor.* Paper presented at the annual meeting of National Council of Measurement in Education, Seattle, WA.

Landauer, T. K., & Dumais, S. T. (1997). A solution to Plato's problem: The latent semantic analysis theory of acquisition, induction, and representation of knowledge. *Psychological Review, 104,* 211–240.

Landauer, T. K., Foltz, P. W., & Laham, D. (1998). An introduction to latent semantic analysis. *Discourse Processes, 25,* 259–284.

Landauer, T. K., Laham, D., & Foltz, P. W. (2000). The Intelligent Essay Assessor. *IEEE Intelligent Systems, 15*(5), 27–31. Retrieved May 6, 2002, from http://www.computer.org/intelligent/ex2000/pdf/x5022.pdf

Landauer, T. K., Laham, D., & Foltz, P. W. (2001, February). *The intelligent essay assessor: Putting knowledge to the test.* Paper presented at the Association of Test Publishers Computer-Based Testing: Emerging Technologies and Opportunities for Diverse Applications conference, Tucson, AZ.

Messick, S. (1988). The once and future issues of validity: Assessing the meaning and consequences of measurement. In H. Wainer & H. Braun (Eds.), *Test validity* (pp. 33–48). Hillsdale, NJ: Lawrence Erlbaum Associates, Inc.

Messick, S. (1989). Validity. In R. L. Linn (Ed.), *Educational measurement* (pp. 13–103). Phoenix, AZ: The Oryx Press.

Messick, S. (1995). Validity of psychological assessment: Validation of inferences from person's responses and performances as scientific inquiry into score meaning. *American Psychologists, 50,* 741–749.

Mislevy, R. J., Steinberg, L. S., Breyer, F. J., Almond, R. G., & Johnson, L. (2002/this issue). Making sense of data from complex assessments. *Applied Measurement in Education, 15,* 363–389.

Page, E. B. (1966). The imminence of grading essays by computer. *Phi Delta Kappan, 48,* 238–243.

Page, E. B. (1994). Computer grading of student prose, using modern concepts and software. *Journal of Experimental Education, 62,* 127–142.

Page, E. B., & Petersen, N. S. (1995). The computer moves into essay grading: updating the ancient test. *Phi Delta Kappan, 77,* 561–565.

Page, E. B., Poggio, J. P., & Keith, T. Z. (1997, March). *Computer analysis of student essays: finding trait differences in student profile.* Paper presented at the annual meeting of the American Educational Research Association, Chicago.

Powers, D. E., Burstein, J. C., Chodorow, M., Fowles, M. E., & Kukich, K. (2001, March). *Stumping e-rater: Challenging the validity of automated essay scoring* (GRE Board Professional Rep. No. 98–08bP, ETS Research Rep. No. 01–03). Princeton, NJ: Educational Testing Service. Retrieved May 6, 2002, from http://www.ets.org/research/dload/powers_0103.pdf

Sebrechts, M. M. (1992). From testing to training: Evaluating automated diagnosis in statistics and algebra. In C. Frasson, G. Gauthier, & G. I. McCalla (Eds.), *Intelligent tutoring systems* (pp. 560–566). Hiedelberg, Germany: Springer-Verlag.

Shermis, M. D. (2001, February). *Automated essay scoring: Overview and future direction.* Paper presented at the Association of Test Publishers Computer-Based Testing: Emerging Technologies and Opportunities for Diverse Applications conference, Tucson, AZ.

Shermis, M. D., Koch, C. M., Page, E. B., Keith, T. Z., & Harrington, S. (1999, April). *Trait ratings for automated essay grading.* Paper presented at the annual meeting of National Council on Measurement in Education, Montreal, Canada.

Shermis, M. D., Rasmussen, J. L., Rajecki, D. W., Olson, J., & Marsiglio, C. (2001). All prompts are not created equal, but some prompts are more equal than others. *Journal of Applied Measurement, 2,* 153–169.

Traub, R. E. (1994). *Reliability for the social sciences: Theory and applications.* Thousand Oaks, CA: Sage.

Williamson, D. M., Bejar, I. I., & Hone, A. S. (1999). "Mental model" comparison of automated and human scoring. *Journal of Educational Measurement, 36,* 158–184.

APPLIED MEASUREMENT IN EDUCATION, *15*(4), 413–432

Validity Issues for Performance-Based Tests Scored With Computer-Automated Scoring Systems

Brian E. Clauser
National Board of Medical Examiners
Philadelphia, PA

Michael T. Kane
National Conference of Bar Examiners
Madison, WI

David B. Swanson
National Board of Medical Examiners
Philadelphia, PA

With the increasing use of automated scoring systems in high-stakes testing, it has become essential that test developers assess the validity of the inferences based on scores produced by these systems. In this article, we attempt to place the issues associated with computer-automated scoring within the context of current validity theory. Although it is assumed that the criteria appropriate for evaluating the validity of score interpretations are the same for tests using automated scoring procedures as for other assessments, different aspects of the validity argument may require emphasis as a function of the scoring procedure. We begin the article with a taxonomy of automated scoring procedures. The presentation of this taxonomy provides a framework for discussing threats to validity that may take on increased importance for specific approaches to automated scoring. We then present a general discussion of the process by which test-based inferences are validated, followed by a discussion of the special issues that must be considered when scoring is done by computer.

The increasing use of computers for test delivery has the potential to greatly expand the range of performance tasks included in standardized assessments. Taking

---

Requests for reprints should be sent to Brian E. Clauser, National Board of Medical Examiners, 3750 Market Street, Philadelphia, PA 19104. E-mail: bclauser@nbme.org

advantage of multimedia and the dynamic computer interface to better assess examinee proficiencies has obvious appeal. However, for these alternative formats to be efficient, it will be necessary for the computer not only to deliver these complex assessments but also to score them.

In response to this need for efficient scoring procedures, considerable research has focused on the development of automated systems to score complex computer-delivered formats. Automated systems have been developed for scoring essays (Landauer, Laham, & Foltz, 2001; Page & Petersen, 1995) as well as computer-based measures of architectural problem solving (Bejar & Braun, 1999), computer programming (Braun, Bennett, Frye, & Soloway, 1990), mathematics (Bennett & Sebrechts, 1996; Sebrechts, Bennett, & Rock, 1991), hypothesis formulation (Kaplan & Bennett, 1994) and physicians' patient management (Clauser, Margolis, Clyman, & Ross, 1997). Although some of these systems are at the prototype stage, others are in operational use. With the increasing use of automated scoring systems in high-stakes testing, it has become essential that test developers assess the validity of the inferences based on scores produced by these systems.

Although test validity has been a matter of concern for generations, if not millennia (Dubois, 1970), automated scoring introduces new problems. In this article we attempt to place the issues associated with computer-automated scoring within the context of current validity theory. Although it is assumed that the criteria appropriate for evaluating the validity of score interpretations are the same for tests using automated scoring procedures as for other assessments, different aspects of the validity argument may require emphasis as a function of the scoring procedure.

We begin this article with a taxonomy of automated scoring procedures. The presentation of this taxonomy provides a framework for discussing threats to validity that may take on increased importance for specific approaches to automated scoring. We then present a general discussion of the process by which test-based inferences are validated, followed by a discussion of the special issues that must be considered when scoring is done by computer.

A TAXONOMY OF AUTOMATED
SCORING PROCEDURES

The taxonomy intends to serve two purposes. First, it provides a framework for the subsequent analysis of threats to validity. As we discuss in the following sections, the specifics of the validity argument will depend on the methodology used in developing the scoring procedure. In addition, the taxonomy provides at least an implicit definition of what is meant in this article by computer-automated scoring systems.

The taxonomy, presented in Table 1, organizes potential procedures in terms of two dimensions. The primary dimension, represented by the vertical axis, categorizes procedures based on the methodology used to extract and operationalize the

TABLE 1
A Taxonomy of Approaches to Automated Scoring

	Focus of the Scoring Model	
Basis for Model	Process	Product/Outcome
Expert-articulated rules or criteria	Rule-based scoring of simulations of physicians' patient-management skills[a]	Scoring of computerized architectural problem[b]
Rules inferred from expert ratings of examinee performance		
AI models of expert ratings		AI approaches to essay scoring trained on essays rated by experts[c]
Regression-based models of expert ratings	Regression-based scoring of simulations of physicians' patient-management skills[d]	
Models based on expert performance on assessment tasks	"Aggregate scoring" of simulations of physicians' patient-management skills[e]	AI approaches to essay scoring trained on essays produced by experts[c]
Rules or criteria based on psychological models of tasks or performance	Scoring of dental simulations[f]	

Note. AI = artificial intelligence.

[a]See Clauser, Ross, et al. (1997). [b]See Bejar (1991) and Bejar and Braun (1999). [c]See Landauer, Laham, and Foltz (in press). [d]See Clauser, Margolis, Clyman, and Ross (1997). [e]See Norman et al. (1989) and Webster, Shea, Norcini, Gross, and Swanson (1988). [f]See Mislevy, Steinberg, Breyer, Almond, and Johnson (2002).

expert knowledge and judgment supporting the scoring procedure. The categories in this dimension include conditions in which (a) experts directly articulate the rules or criteria used to evaluate examinee performance, (b) some inferential process is used to identify rules or criteria used by experts in rating examinee performance, (c) some inferential process is used to identify rules or criteria from expert performance of the task, or (d) the rules or criteria follow from some psychological model of tasks or performance and the role of the expert is to apply the model in the particular context.

The horizontal axis in Table 1 represents the focus of the scoring procedure—namely, whether the score is to be an evaluation of the process used by the examinee or of the product or outcome of the performance. In principle, any of the cells produced by crossing the two axes provide a potentially legitimate scoring approach. In practice, some combinations are much more common than others. Examples of approaches representing several of the cells are included in Table 1 and are described here to further elucidate the taxonomy.

Expert-Articulated Scoring Criteria

Perhaps the most common approach to the development of automated scoring systems is represented by the cell for expert-articulated criteria applied to a product or outcome. A variety of innovative item formats use this approach, including the mathematical expression response type proposed by Bennett, Steffen, Singley, Morley, and Jacquemin (1997) and the formulating-hypothesis item type described by Kaplan and Bennett (1994). With the mathematical expression response type, the examinee is given a verbal description ("During one week in Trenton in January, it snowed on s days and was fair on the other days. ... What is the probability that a randomly selected day from that week was fair?" [p. 164]) and asked to produce a mathematical expression that represents the answer. The difficulty in scoring this type of item is that there are an unlimited number of equivalent ways of expressing the same relationship, such as

$$1-\frac{s}{7} \tag{1}$$

vs.

$$\frac{7-s}{7}. \tag{2}$$

In this case, scoring requires the computer to apply the expert-articulated criterion represented by the simple rule, "All expressions mathematically equivalent to expression (1) are correct."

More elaborate examples of this approach to scoring are provided by Bejar (1995) in the context of scoring architectural problems. For example, an examinee may be required to design the grading around a building to ensure run-off. The expert-articulated criteria may require that little or no pooling would result during a rainstorm. The computer may then evaluate the design produced by an examinee using an algorithm that simulates the effects of a rainstorm. In this case, the criterion is reasonably simple, its application is complex. By contrast, other architectural tasks are scored using elaborate decision trees (Bejar, 1995). The design is broken down into specific measurable or definable features. To use the simple example of creating a design for a bathroom, the scoring tree could define the performance in terms of the placement of fixtures (toilet, bathtub, sink), cabinets, and lights. In addition to evaluating the design in terms of the presence or absence of each of the features, scoring may include orientation, clearance, and proximity to other features.

The methodologies described in the previous paragraphs all apply expert-articulated criteria to the evaluation of a product or outcome. Such rules can also be applied to the evaluation of a process, exemplified in the work of Clauser, Ross, and colleagues (1997) in assessing physicians' patient management within a simulated patient care environment. Scoring was based on rules produced by a committee of experts that mapped patterns of actions, sequence, and timing into specified score categories. Scoring focused on process rather than outcome in the sense that an examinee who effectively treated the patient without completing the diagnostic steps necessary to justify the treatment could receive a low score even though the patient outcome would have been positive. Clearly, an outcome-based evaluation would be possible in this context, but the choice between process and outcome would have a significant impact on the interpretation of the resulting score.

Inferences From Expert Ratings

The history of efforts to produce algorithms that can replace expert judges with statistical inference predates computers. Early in the 20th century, both Pearson (1915) and Thorndike (1918) argued that it should be possible to produce statistical algorithms that would improve on human judgments. Meehl (1954) demonstrated that reasonably simple statistical procedures, modeled on expert ratings, could outperform experts. Given this history, it is not surprising that researchers would consider this approach in developing scoring algorithms intended to replace expert raters.

One example of this approach, again focusing on process, comes from the work of Clauser, Margolis, Clyman, and Ross (1997), who used a regression-based procedure to weight scorable units from a patient management simulation to produce scores that could replace expert ratings of the same performance. With this procedure, a sample of examinee performances is selected, and ratings are produced by experts. These ratings then serve as the dependent variable in a regression analysis, with computer-scorable aspects of examinee performance serving as the independent variables.

Similar approaches have been used in contexts in which the focus of the evaluation is a product rather than a process. For example, Page (1966) and Page and Petersen (1995) reported on regression-based procedures for scoring essays. Essay scoring has received considerable attention, and in addition to regression-based models, artificial-intelligence-based approaches have been developed in which more complex procedures are used (see Landauer et al., 2001, for an example).

Models Based on Expert Performance

Table 1 also lists a category representing inferred models based on expert performance (as opposed to expert judgment). Again, this approach to scoring performance assessments has a history that predates computerized scoring applications.

The concept is that rather than asking experts to explain what constitutes good performance or asking experts to make judgments about the merit of specific performances, experts are asked to actually perform the assessment task. Expert performance then becomes the criterion. An early example of this methodology was presented by Rimoldi (1955) as an approach to evaluating problem-solving skills. Rimoldi's work focused on the process of decision making. More recently, this general approach has been applied to the scoring of essays (again, see Landauer et al., 2001). As with most other essay scoring, this approach focused on evaluation of the product.

Criteria Based on Psychological Models

A final broad category of scoring methodologies is that in which the procedure is driven by some psychological model or theory. Recent work by Mislevy and colleagues (e.g., Mislevy, Steinberg, Breyer, Almond, & Johnson, 2002) is representative of this approach. With this approach, a cognitive psychological framework is used to define levels of performance (i.e., cognitive development). A combination of expert-articulated rules and statistical estimation techniques is then used to build the scoring procedure. Although the example presented in this issue focuses on the evaluation of the process used by dental hygienists, in principle this approach could evaluate either a process or product.

The preceding paragraphs should make it clear that the variety of automated scoring procedures already in use or under development is considerable and that this range is likely to continue to grow rapidly. Several of these applications are already used in large-scale, high-stakes contexts. The widening use of these procedures highlights the importance of considering the validity issues associated with these applications. In the next section, we outline a general framework for validity arguments and then consider the use of these scoring systems within that framework.

VALIDITY

The new *Standards for Educational and Psychological Testing* (AERA/APA/NCME, 1999) defines validity as "the degree to which evidence and theory support the interpretation of test scores entailed by proposed uses" (p. 9) and treats validation as the development of evidence providing "a sound scientific basis for the proposed score interpretations" (p. 9).

The process of developing support for a proposed interpretation involves the development of a coherent argument for the interpretation (Cronbach, 1988; House, 1980). The *validity argument* provides an overall evaluation of the plausibility of the intended interpretation (Cronbach, 1988). It includes the evidence for and against the proposed interpretation and evidence for or against plausible alternate interpretations.

To develop a coherent argument for a proposed interpretation, it is necessary to have a clear understanding of the interpretation. The interpretation of the test scores can be represented as a chain or network of inferences leading from the test scores to the conclusions to be drawn and any decisions to be based on these conclusions (Crooks, Kane, & Cohen, 1996; Kane, 1992; Shepard, 1993). This *interpretive argument* provides an explicit statement of the inferences and assumptions inherent in the interpretation and provides a framework for evaluating the proposed interpretation in some detail.

The validity argument provides a systematic evaluation of the inferences and assumptions identified in the interpretive argument, paying particular attention to the weakest parts of this argument. All of the inferences and assumptions must be sound if the interpretative argument is to be considered valid, and therefore, the plausibility of the interpretation is determined by the plausibility of its weakest links (Cronbach, 1971; Messick, 1989). Evidence that provides further support for a highly plausible assumption does not add much to the overall plausibility of the argument. Evidence relevant to the most questionable inferences in the interpretive argument provides the most effective contribution to the validity argument. All of the inferences and assumptions in the interpretative argument must hold for the proposed interpretation to be considered valid.

Several general types of inferences and assumptions appear in interpretive arguments.

1. The acceptance of a number as a test score assumes that the number was assigned using appropriate procedures.
2. Generalizations from the observed score to the expected score over some universe of possible observations rest on assumptions about the invariance of observed scores over different conditions of observation.
3. Extrapolations beyond the testing context are based on assumptions about the relationship between the performances observed during the assessment and the ("real-world") performances of ultimate interest.
4. Any theory-based inferences assume that the theory is credible.
5. The decisions based on test scores make assumptions about the desirability of various kinds of outcomes—that is, about values and consequences.

These five types of arguments are referred to by Kane, Crooks, and Cohen (1999) as evaluation, generalization, extrapolation, explanation, and decision.

Evaluation

This stage of the argument may be thought of as focusing on accuracy of implementation. Adherence to the conditions of standardization and accuracy of scoring are central issues. Particularly with performance assessments, where the complexity of standardization of administration is likely to increase with the complexity of the task, assessments administered on computer may have an advantage. Computer delivery should allow for greater control over extraneous variables in test administration (provided software and hardware used in delivery are standardized).

In terms of scoring accuracy, scores produced by an automated scoring system will replace those of a human rater. Following this logic, numerous studies have focused on demonstrating the correspondence between scores produced by computerized procedures and expert ratings of the same performances (Bejar, 1991; Bennett & Sebrechts, 1994; Braun, Bennett, Frye, & Soloway, 1990; Clauser, Margolis, et al., 1997; Clauser et al., 1995; Kaplan & Bennett, 1994; Page & Petersen, 1995; Sebrechts, Bennett, & Rock, 1991).

Although previous authors (e.g., Bejar & Bennett, 1997) have argued that the validity argument for scores produced by automated systems must go beyond demonstration of the correspondence between scores and ratings, the majority of early studies of these systems have had exactly this focus. Closer consideration of this type of validity evidence suggests that this is not always necessary and is generally not sufficient. It is not necessary in those cases in which the scoring rule is based on expert-articulated criteria. As Williamson, Bejar, and Hone (1999) pointed out, it is possible for the machine to implement accepted criteria more accurately than raters can implement these same criteria, making adherence to the criteria rather than correspondence with the ratings of judges the standard of interest. It is not sufficient because the decision to use computer-automated scoring may have ripple effects that extend through each step in the argument.

Generalization

The second step in the argument intends to support the credibility of the intended generalizations of the scores. In the context of performance assessment, the usual concerns include generalization over tasks and raters. This might sensibly be extended to include generalization over occasions on which the task could have been completed and occasions on which the raters could have scored the task.

Rater Error. The introduction of automated scoring clearly impacts the portion of the argument that would otherwise focus on rater-related error. One way to view this is to see the replacement of raters with a computer as the elimination of random error at the possible expense of introducing systematic error. Using a computerized scoring system eliminates the random errors that would be associated with differences among raters (or in the case of procedures that use multiple raters, differences among sets of raters). It also eliminates differences that would be associated with rating occasions. It is almost inevitable that when a rater rates the same set of performances on multiple occasions, there will be some differences in the scores assigned. These fluctuations may represent trends in which the rater becomes more or less lenient over time or they may be the result of inattention (or inconsistent attention to detail). The automated system eliminates these fluctuations by uniformly and mechanically applying the scoring criteria.

Although mechanical uniformity has appeal, the appeal is limited by the extent to which the user can be satisfied that the resulting score accurately represents the quality of the performance. Several issues related to generalization remain. First, when automated scoring systems are developed, the algorithms are guided by or modeled on the opinions of a sample of experts on a sample of occasions. Although in practice a single group of experts will typically develop an algorithm, which will then be used to score all examinees, the universe of generalization is likely to be at least as broad as the set of all algorithms produced by an unlimited number of groups of equally qualified experts, each following the same procedure for algorithm development. Beyond this, it is sensible to view the intended generalization as across scores produced by algorithms developed by qualified experts using similar (but not identical) procedures for algorithm development. Because for operational use there will typically be only a single scoring algorithm for each task, the impact of these sources of variability will be systematic. Because these effects will be confounded with other aspects of the task, it will generally be impossible to account for them.

There is relatively little literature describing research on these issues. Clauser, Harik, and Clyman (2000) published the results of a generalizability analysis designed to compare computer-based scores produced by independent groups of experts. The scoring algorithms for these computer-based case simulations, designed to assess physicians' patient management skills, were developed using a regression-based policy-capturing procedure. Three independent and equivalent groups of experts each participated in the development of scoring algorithms for the same four tasks. A data set was then produced that included three scores (one from each algorithm) for each of the examinees on each of the four tasks. Generalizability analysis of this data set indicated that, although groups may differ in leniency, after scaling, the group effect introduced relatively little error into the scores. Universe score correlations (estimated true-score correlations) were approximately unity, suggesting that the different algorithms were measuring the same underlying trait. This study provides an example of the type of evidence that might support generalization across automated scoring systems developed by randomly equivalent groups of experts using the same development procedure. Generalization across different, but possibly equivalent, scoring procedures is a somewhat more complex problem.

Of interest in examining generalization across scoring systems is verification that alternative procedures are actually measuring the same underlying proficiency or composite and that apparently inconsequential implementation decisions are in fact inconsequential. Of concern in this context is the possibility that these apparently minor aspects of the scoring procedure could introduce systematic errors in scores. Clauser, Swanson, and Clyman (1999) presented a comparison of ratings and scores produced using two different computerized scoring systems. Estimated true-score correlations were calculated to assess the extent to which the scores produced with the computerized algorithms assessed the same proficiency as the corresponding ratings. Results reported in that article show true correlations (disattenuated for measurement error) between computer-produced scores and the ratings approximating unity (0.98–1.00). An additional analysis, not previously reported, showed the scores from the two different computerized algorithms had a true correlation of 1.00. In the context of the article, Clauser et al. (1999) presented these results to support their interpretations of differences in generalizability across scoring methods. In the context of the broader validity argument, these results are important because they argue against the presence of systematic, scoring-system-specific variance in the scores.

Although the term *trait* carries connotations that might best be avoided, one way of conceptualizing and examining the problem is within the framework of Campbell and Fiske's (1959) multitrait–multimethod matrix. The type of trait-irrelevant, scoring-system-specific variance that this type of analysis could identify is problematic for two reasons. First, it contributes to measurement error. Second, because it is common across tasks, this source of error may be mistaken for true-score or universe-score variance, leading to inflated estimates of measurement precision.

Task Specificity.   To this point, discussion has focused on those issues in the generalizability of scores from automated scoring systems that have analogues in the rater effects present in performance assessments scored by expert raters (e.g., rater, rater by task, rater by examinee, rater by task by examinee). Automated scoring systems may also impact task specificity, typically represented in a generalizability theory framework in terms of the person-by-task effect and higher order interactions.

Regardless of the methodological framework used to develop the scoring algorithm, the specific decisions made in developing the algorithm may lead to a score that better generalizes across tasks or that focuses on the specifics of the individual task. The generalizability of scores across tasks must be evaluated. Studies that strictly focus on the correlation (or other correspondence) between candidate scores on an individual task and a criterion (e.g., expert rating of the same performance) do not provide an evaluation of task-to-task variability in the scores. The automated score may be disproportionately capturing aspects of the criterion variance that do not generalize across tasks. Clauser and Clyman (1999) reported the results of a study evaluating a scoring procedure using regression-based modeling, explicitly designed to maximize the shared variance across tasks (additional details follow). Although results indicated that the specific strategy examined in the Clauser and Clyman study may have increased generalizability by capturing construct irrelevant variance, the logic of this approach underscores that it may be possible to increase the construct-relevant variance at the expense of task-specific variance.

This potential for enhancing generalizability with appropriately engineered automated scoring systems offers promise. However, it should be noted that a serious tradeoff exists between the evaluation and generalization steps in terms of the potential impact of an automated scoring system. The automated scoring system may substantially improve generalizability by eliminating random errors due to rater effects, rater–examinee interactions, rater–rating occasion interaction, and rater–examinee–rating occasion interaction. It may also help to reduce the task specificity. However, the automated scoring system may also add systematic errors by introducing consistent construct-irrelevant factors into the evaluation of examinee performances. Systematic errors tend to be more damaging than random errors because they do not average out. Nevertheless, a relatively small increase in systematic error accompanied by a relatively large decrease in random error can be a good tradeoff in many contexts.

Extrapolation

The third step in the argument is extrapolation. The issue here focuses on linking the conditions under which the data were collected to other, possibly more realistic or relevant conditions. This is likely to be an important step in the validation process for computer-delivered assessments. Simulations that stop short of producing a completely faithful reproduction of reality unavoidably lead to questions about the extent to which departures from reality (e.g., the limitations of the interface, features of the environment not present in the simulation) influence the resulting measure. In this situation, the underlying logic supporting the validity argument must rest on the assumption that the assessment tasks relate to a necessary, but perhaps not sufficient, set of assessment criteria.

The importance (necessity) of the central features of this type of assessment task may be established directly through appeal to content considerations. It is more difficult to demonstrate that the score does not additionally reflect systematic but construct irrelevant variance. One obvious potential concern is familiarity (or lack of familiarity) with the software interface, but other aspects of the way examinees interact with the simulation may also have a systematic impact on scores. For example, response styles may differ across examinees in ways that do not generalize to examinee behavior in an actual practice setting. An examinee that is highly efficient (or tediously thorough) in managing a simulated patient in an assessment may not perform similarly in actual practice.

Behavior patterns of this sort may be artifacts of the testing format, but it is clear that decisions about scoring could accentuate or minimize the impact of these artifacts. For example, a scoring system for a patient management simulation that simply computed the number of appropriate medical interventions recorded on a simulated order sheet might penalize examinees who are highly efficient in reaching a diagnosis.

Explanation

The fourth aspect of the validity argument focuses on the extent to which scores are useful for explaining examinee performance. Some decisions made in development of the scoring procedure will have an obvious impact on how scores can be interpreted. For example, some automated scoring systems are specifically developed to provide diagnostic feedback along with recommendations for improving performance. In addition, scoring systems can be developed based on a cognitive model for the proficiency of interest. To the extent that the model is useful, this framework would presumably enhance the utility of the scores for explanatory purposes.

Automated scoring systems can be especially appealing for diagnostic assessments based on complex performance models. If the performance on each task is postulated to be a function of a number of component skills (Tatsuoka, 1990), the best estimate of an examinee's level of competence on a component skill may be a weighted function of their performance over all tasks on the assessment. Assuming that the number of component skills is fairly large, as it often is, and the number of tasks is substantial, as it may need to be to provide separate estimates of all component skills, automated scoring may be the only feasible option, just because of the complexity of the required record keeping.

Decision

The final step in the argument focuses on the dependability of decisions made using the scores. Without the first four stages of the argument, this last step is clearly untenable. However, again, choices made in developing the scoring algorithm may have an important impact on the strength of this aspect of the argument. Consider a test for licensure or certification, in which the purpose of the decision is to identify practitioners who have the necessary skills to perform safely and competently in some profession. Clearly, the scoring system must focus on the proficiency of interest, but if it is further focused on the specific types of behaviors that are likely to be critical in separating competent from incompetent practitioners, the argument will be strengthened. Although this may seem obvious, accomplishing this goal is likely to be far from simple. Presumably, for more challenging tasks it will be desirable for the scoring system to focus on simpler aspects of task performance and the reverse may be true for less difficult tasks. For a licensure examination, it is also important that the scoring focus on aspects of performance most closely related to public safety. Unfortunately, identifying scoring points that are both highly discriminating and have a prespecified level of difficulty is not likely to be any easier than controlling the difficulty and discrimination of multiple-choice questions. To be useful, test developers will need to make judgments that satisfy content experts and can be empirically related to pass–fail decisions. This is no simple accomplishment.

As discussed earlier in connection with the relationship between scoring algorithms and the use of performance models for explanation, the adoption of such models can make it easier to develop scoring algorithms and at the same time make their use almost essential. The models can facilitate the development of the scoring algorithms by suggesting specific, well-defined scoring criteria for pass-fail decisions. For example, if the model indicates that competent performers will engage in several essential steps in performing the task, then a performance involving these steps in the proper sequence would get a passing grade, while a performance omitting one or more essential steps would get a failing grade.

The scoring rules coming out of models of competence are likely to be complicated because most real-world problems can be solved in more than one way, and the scoring algorithm will have to appropriately reward all legitimate solutions. To the extent that the scoring rules suggested by the model of competence are complex, involving the monitoring of a number of possible sequences of steps, scoring by human raters is likely to be error prone, and automated scoring procedures may be especially appealing.

As with other steps in the interpretative argument, the potential impact of construct-irrelevant variance impacts this stage of the argument as well. If scores produced by the scoring algorithm reflect aspects of the performance not relevant to the intended interpretation of the scores, examinees may be able to exploit this to improve their scores and alter the decisions. For example, some early approaches to scoring essays included scoring variables such as the total number of words, the number of words per sentence, and the number of syllables per word. Examinees could easily be coached to increase these counts, and their scores, without improving their writing. This example is particularly relevant because it highlights the fact that efforts to identify easily quantifiable aspects of performance may lead to reliance on variables that include construct-irrelevant variance.

Unique Threats to Validity

In the previous sections, we presented a discussion of threats to validity that require attention regardless of how the automated scoring algorithm was developed. In the following sections, we focus this discussion by examining some special issues that arise as a function of the methodology used to develop the scoring procedure.

Expert-Articulated Rules

The obvious strength of scoring systems that rely on expert-articulated rules is that the experts lend credibility to associated content validity arguments. The specific threats to validity that arise in this context follow from the fact that experts are not infallible. To produce a useful scoring system, experts must be able to correctly identify the aspects of a performance that are critical; they must be able to accurately articulate their rules or criteria; and the expert-articulated rules must be correctly translated into computer code. None of these steps is trivial. Although a review of the relevant literature is beyond the scope of this article, it should be noted that research on expert judgment has highlighted these difficulties. Brehmer and Brehmer (1988) reviewed numerous studies describing both limitations in the ability of experts to articulate their criteria and failures to extract and apply information from expert produced protocols. In addition, Dawes, Faust, and Meehl (1989) argued that expert judgment is often limited because it can be influenced by extraneous factors that may then be introduced into the scoring system. (Note, however, that having human raters score all responses does not eliminate the influence of extraneous factors.)

Another important threat to these types of systems is that the definitions or criteria used in the algorithm can be too restrictive. Consider as an example the scoring of the formulating-hypothesis item type (Kaplan & Bennett, 1994) described previously. The logic of this approach is that the constructed responses produced by the examinees are reduced to a semantic base form and matched with a key that represents the correct answers. It is not too difficult to imagine that some particularly clever examinee could come up with a novel but legitimate hypothesis that had not been considered by the experts who defined the key. Such a novel solution would not be recognized by a scoring system that was not programmed for it, but it could be recognized by a human rater. Concern that mechanical scoring procedures may fail to fairly evaluate creative responses has also been a long-standing concern with the use of computers for scoring essays. Although some approaches may reduce the likelihood of this type of error (see Landauer et al., 2001) it remains a matter of concern and an effective interpretative argument must provide evidence that this threat to validity has been controlled.

Rules Inferred From Expert Ratings

In addition to supportive empirical results (Clauser, Margolis, et al., 1997; Dawes & Corrigan, 1974; Dawes et al., 1989), a major attraction of scoring procedures based on rules inferred from expert ratings is that these approaches eliminate the need for experts to articulate their judgment criteria. In addition, insofar as these systems are typically based on the judgments of numerous experts, the impact of extraneous factors influencing individual experts should be reduced.

Unfortunately, although it reduces some of the risks associated with approaches relying on expert articulated rules, the process of inferring rules carries its own risks to validity. Foremost among these is the potential that the inferential procedures may capitalize on aspects of the performance that may correlate with expert judgment for the sample of judges and performances used in developing the scoring algorithm, even though they are construct irrelevant. Relatively little literature is available describing this type of effect.

One example is found in results reported by Clauser and Clyman (1999). Their study (also discussed earlier) evaluated the results of a regression-based scoring procedure intended to improve the generalizability of scores by limiting the impact of task specificity. Their approach used a regression procedure to predict task scores based on quantifiable (computer scorable) aspects of examinee performance. Unlike the approach used in their previous work (e.g., Clauser, Margolis, et al., 1997) in which ratings of the specific task being modeled were used as the dependent variable in developing the regression weights, in this case, the examinee's average rating across all tasks on the test form was used as the criterion. The resulting scores were shown to be more generalizable across tasks, but this increase in generalizability was not accompanied by an increase in the correlation with the criterion (corrected for the reliabilities of the test and criterion). This strongly suggested that the procedure was systematically capturing some source of criterion-irrelevant variance. Unfortunately, the results did not make clear the specifics of this apparent artifact. It was hypothesized that the results may have been sensitive to examinee response patterns that were stable across tasks but largely construct irrelevant, such as a tendency to be thorough as opposed to efficient.

Another threat to validity that should be examined is the appropriateness of the statistical procedures used for making inferences. In the simple (and common) case in which the procedure is based on multiple regression, the potential problems are well known (e.g., overfitting the model because of small sample sizes, drawing inferences when model fit is poor, applying a model built from unrepresentative samples). Assessment of these potential limitations through cross-validation and examination of model fit is reasonably straightforward. The same sorts of problems can be present when more elaborate statistical procedures are used (e.g., artificial neural networks, Bayesian inference networks). Empirical checks similar to those used for multiple regression should also be applied in these instances.

Models Based on Expert Behavior

There are differing approaches to modeling expert behavior, and the specific threats to validity posed by each of these vary to some degree. For example, expert behavior could provide the basis for development of automated scoring algorithms by using "think aloud" procedures in which the experts work their way through the task and describe what they are doing and why. (Although the authors are unaware of any computer-automated scoring procedures that are based on this approach, they have been used in the past to develop scoring rules for assessment formats such as paper-and-pencil-based patient management problems.) Because this approach depends on the translation of experts' explanation of their behavior into a usable algorithm, it is potentially vulnerable to the same risks described in the context of approaches based on expert-articulated rules. Alternatively, statistical procedures can be used to infer scoring criteria using expert performance as the model (e.g., Landauer et al., 2001. This approach can be vulnerable to some of the same threats to validity previously described in the context of procedures based on inferences from expert ratings.

Regardless of which approach is used to model expert behavior, use of expert behavior as the basis for modeling introduces some unique risks. Particularly in a context in which scores are intended to reflect process rather than product or outcome, the use of an expert model may be problematic. Consider, as an example, physician patient management. It is well known that highly experienced practitioners may follow a different (more efficient) process in diagnosing a patient than that taught to (and, it is hoped, used by) the beginning practitioner (Swanson, Norman, & Linn, 1995). If scoring criteria are modeled on the behavior of the experienced expert, they may not be fully appropriate for use in the assessment of students or beginning practitioners. Alternatively, if the "experts" are a group of beginning practitioners who have been judged to be competent, the application of scoring rules based on their performance may disadvantage any examinee whose performance was actually similar to that of the experienced practitioner. At a minimum, the potential problem described in this example will make it clear that the experts must be carefully chosen, assessment tasks must be carefully designed, and the interpretation of the resulting scores must be carefully circumscribed.

More generally, the use of expert performances to develop scoring criteria may lead to scoring algorithms that are not very sensitive to the kinds of mistakes made by novices. That is, a scoring algorithm based on expert performance might not differentiate very well between minor mistakes and more serious problems in performance, simply because the experts will make few of either kind of mistake, and as a result the scoring algorithm may not be able to identify the most likely errors of novices. As a result, the assessment might not be very effective in distinguishing a just-competent, beginning practitioner from an incompetent practitioner.

Rules Based on Psychological Models

There is obviously considerable appeal to making use of models of examinee performance to construct scoring procedures. For one thing, the models lead to scores that explain the performance in the framework provided by the model. This approach has the potential to move from scoring as a kind of behavioral checklist in which examinee actions are counted or categorized to a richer level in which the score provides insight into the mental processes underlying the performance. The limitation associated with this methodology is that as the complexity of the inferences increases so does the complexity of the validity argument required to support those inferences.

Clearly, any such approach requires considerable confidence in the cognitive model. In circumstances in which the task is relatively simple (e.g., constructing specified shapes or patterns using colored blocks), there may be compelling empirical evidence to support a cognitive model. In other circumstances, there will not be a single model supported by compelling empirical evidence. If one considers, for example, the literature on clinical problem solving in medicine, there is no shortage of cognitive models. What is missing is an empirically based consensus regarding which model is correct or which model is appropriate for which type of inference. This difficulty is exacerbated because to apply these models, it is not just the general framework that must be accepted, but specifics at a reasonably detailed level.

In some circumstances it may be possible to sidestep this issue by linking the intended interpretation to a selected performance model. However, under conditions in which the test score is the basis for high-stakes decisions, this, in effect, forces the examinee to accept the implications and impact of the selected model. In addition, there are at least some circumstances in which this impact may be systematic, raising serious questions about fairness. If the curriculum or teaching approach varies across schools ("schools of thought" or individual training programs) and that approach is linked to views about the presumed cognitive model underlying expert performance, use of a single performance model may systematically disadvantage examinees trained using a different framework.

Beyond the requirement that the validation argument supports the use of the specific cognitive model selected, it seems important to provide evidence that the model has been implemented appropriately. This implementation will be based on a combination of expert judgment and statistical estimation. An argument supporting the implementation will require both consideration of the extent to which the assumptions supporting the statistical estimation are reasonable in the context of the application and a demonstration that experts are qualified for their task. This latter consideration may be complex because the required expertise is in application of the cognitive model that may go well beyond the practice or content expertise that is typically expected of "experts" in the area under assessment. Decisions made in implementing these models may be less directly linked to observable outcomes or widely acknowledged standards of practice, creating at least the potential appearance of subjectivity.

The types of provisional criteria accessible to researchers examining scoring systems representing other taxonomic approaches may not be feasible with these procedures (e.g., correspondence to ratings of the same performance). For better or worse, the ultimate evidence required to support the efficacy of these scoring procedures is likely to be the usefulness of the resulting scores. Direct evidence of this type might include a demonstration that remediation of failing examinees could occur more quickly and efficiently as a result of the interpretations made based on these scores.

CONCLUDING REMARKS

The practical advantages of using automated scoring systems are clear. The extent to which multiple-choice questions have become ubiquitous during the last half century is largely the result of the fact that they can be efficiently scored. Automated scoring systems have the potential to produce this level of efficiency for a range of complex item types. However, the use of automated scoring systems has the potential not only to enhance score validity but to introduce serious threats to validity.

The introduction of an automated scoring model into an assessment system can have an impact on most, if not all, steps in the interpretive argument. The influence of the scoring system is likely to be most direct and obvious for the evaluation, generalization, and extrapolation steps. Compared to direct scoring by experts, the use of an automated system will eliminate the random errors associated with raters and should, therefore, improve overall generalizability. However, to the extent that the automated scoring system incorporates construct-irrelevant sources of variance, it will also introduce systematic errors. To the extent that the systematic error introduced in the evaluation of examinee performances is small compared to the random error eliminated, the introduction of an automated scoring system can improve validity.

Much of the existing research on automated scoring systems has focused on demonstrating a high level of correspondence between scores produced by automated systems and expert raters. This effort to "validate" the scoring system represents an obvious preliminary step. However, to construct a sound validity argument, a much broader range of evidence is required. In this article, we presented an outline of the potential threats to validity associated with the use of automated scoring procedures and types of evidence that may be needed to respond to those threats. Throughout, we placed emphasis on those aspects of the overall interpretative argument that may be called into question by the use of automated scoring systems. The specifics of these arguments will no doubt become more sophisticated as researchers and practitioners gain experience with automated scoring systems. It is hoped that the framework presented here is useful in this process.

REFERENCES

American Educational Research Association, American Psychological Association, and National Council on Measurement in Education. (1999). *Standards for educational and psychological testing*. Washington, DC: Author.

Bejar, I. I. (1991). A methodology for scoring open-ended architectural design problems. *Journal of Applied Psychology, 76*, 522–532.

Bejar I. I. (1995). From adaptive testing to automated scoring of architectural simulations. In E. L. Mancall & P. G. Bashook (Eds.), *Assessing clinical reasoning: The oral examination and alternative methods* (pp. 115–130). Evanston, IL: American Board of Medical Specialties.

Bejar, I. I., & Bennett, R. E. (1997, March). *Validity and automated scoring: It's not only the scoring*. Paper presented at the meeting of the National Council on Measurement in Education, Chicago.

Bejar, I. I., & Braun, H. I. (1999). *Architectural simulations: From research to implementation*. (Research Memorandum RM–99–2). Princeton, NJ: Educational Testing Service.

Bennett, R. E., & Sebrechts, M. M. (1996). The accuracy of expert-system diagnoses of mathematical problem solutions. *Applied Measurement in Education, 9*, 133–150.

Bennett, R. E., Steffen, M., Singley, M. K., Morley, M., & Jacquemin, D. (1997). Evaluating an automatically scorable, open-ended response type for measuring mathematical reasoning in computer-adaptive testing. *Journal of Educational Measurement, 34*, 162–176.

Braun, H. I., Bennett, R. E., Frye, D., & Soloway, E. (1990). Scoring constructed responses using expert systems. *Journal of Educational Measurement, 27*, 93–108.

Brehmer, A., & Brehmer, B. (1988). What have we learned about human judgment from thirty years of policy capturing? In B. Brehmer & C. R. B. Joyce (Eds.), *Human judgment* (pp. 75–114). New York: Holland-North.

Campbell, D. T., & Fiske, D. W. (1959). Convergent and discriminant validation by the Multitrait–multimethod matrix. *Psychological Bulletin, 56*, 81–105.

Clauser, B. E., & Clyman, S. G. (1999, April). *A strategy for increasing the generalizability of scores for performance assessments scored with automated scoring algorithms.* Paper presented at the meeting of the American Educational Research Association, Montreal, Canada.

Clauser, B. E., Harik, P., & Clyman, S. G. (2000). The generalizability of scores for a performance assessment scored with a computer-automated scoring system. *Journal of Educational Measurement,37*, 245–262.

Clauser, B. E., Margolis, M. J., Clyman, S. G., & Ross, L. P. (1997). Development of automated scoring algorithms for complex performance assessments: A comparison of two approaches. *Journal of Educational Measurement, 34*, 141–161.

Clauser, B. E., Ross, L. P., Clyman, S. G., Rose, K. M., Margolis, M. J., Nungester, R. J., et al. (1997). Developing a scoring algorithm to replace expert rating for scoring a complex performance based assessment. *Applied Measurement in Education, 10*, 345–358.

Clauser, B. E., Subhiyah, R. G., Nungester, R. J., Ripkey, D. R., Clyman, S. G., McKinley, D. (1995). Scoring a performance-based assessment by modeling the judgments of experts. *Journal of Educational Measurement, 32*, 397–415.

Clauser, B. E., Swanson, D. B, & Clyman, S. G. (1999). A comparison of the generalizability of scores produced by expert raters and automated scoring systems. *Applied Measurement in Education, 12*, 281–299.

Cronbach, L. J. (1971). Test validation. In R. L. Thorndike (Ed.), *Educational measurement* (2nd ed., pp. 443–507). Washington, DC: American Council on Education.

Cronbach, L. J. (1988). Five perspectives on validity argument. In H. Wainer & H. Braun (Eds.), *Test validity* (pp. 3–17). Hillsdale, NJ: Lawrence Erlbaum Associates, Inc.

Crooks, T., Kane, M., & Cohen, A. (1996). Threats to validity. *Assessment in Education, 3*, 265–285.

Dawes, R. M., & Corrigan, B. (1974). Linear models in decision making. *Psychological Bulletin, 81*, 95–106.

Dawes, R. M., Faust, D., & Meehl, P. E. (1989). Clinical versus actuarial judgment. *Science, 243*, 1668–1674.

Dubois, P. H. (1970). *A history of psychological testing*. Boston: Allyn & Bacon.

House, E. R. (1980). *Evaluating with validity*. Beverly Hills, CA: Sage.

Kane, M. (1992). An argument-based approach to validation. *Psychological Bulletin, 112*, 527–535.

Kane, M., Crooks, T., Cohen, A. (1999). Validating measures of performance. *Educational Measurement: Issues and Practice, 18*(2), 5–17.

Kaplan, R. M., & Bennett, R. E. (1994). *Using a free-response scoring tool to automatically score the formulating-hypotheses item* (RR 94–08). Princeton, NJ: Educational Testing Service.

Landauer, T. K., Laham, D., & Foltz, P. W. (2001). *Automatic essay assessment with Latent Semantic Analysis*. Unpublished manuscript.

Meehl, P. E. (1954). *Clinical versus statistical prediction*. Minneapolis: University of Minnesota Press.

Messick, S. (1989). Validity. In R. L. Linn (Ed.), *Educational measurement* (3rd ed., pp. 13–103). New York: American Council on Education.

Mislevy, R. J., Steinberg, L. S., Breyer, F. J., Almond, R. G., & Johnson, L. (2002/this issue). Making sense of data from complex assessments. *Applied Measurement in Education.*

Norman, G. R., Davis, D. A., Painvin, A., Lindsay, E., Rath, D., & Ragbeer, M. (1989). Comprehensive assessment of clinical competence of family/general physicians using multiple measures. In W. K. Davis (Ed.), *Proceedings of the twenty-eighth annual conference of research in medical education* (pp. 75–80). Washington, DC: Association of American Medical Colleges.

Page, E. B. (1966). Grading essays by computer: Progress report. In J. C. Stanley (Ed.), *Proceedings of the 1966 invitational conference on testing* (pp. 87–100). Princeton, NJ: Educational Testing Service.

Page, E. B., & Petersen, N. S. (1995). The computer moves into essay grading. *Phi Delta Kappan, 76,* 561–565.

Pearson, K. (1915). On the problem of sexing osteometric material. *Biometrika, 10,* 479–487.

Rimoldi, H. J. A. (1955). A technique for the study of problem solving. *Educational and Psychological Measurement, 15,* 450–461.

Sebrechts, M. M., Bennett, R. E., & Rock, D. A. (1991). Agreement between expert-system and human raters on complex constructed-response quantitative items. *Journal of Applied Psychology, 76,* 856–862.

Shepard, L. A. (1993). Evaluating test validity. In L. Darling-Hammond (Ed.), *Review of research in education* (Vol. 19, pp. 405–450). Washington, DC: American Educational Research Association.

Swanson, D. B., Norman, G. R., & Linn, R. (1995). Performance-based assessment: Lessons from the health professions. *Educational Researcher, 24*(5), 5–11, 35

Tatsuoka, K. K. (1990). Toward an integration of item-response theory and cognitive error diagnosis. In N. Frederiksen, R. Glaser, A. Lesgold, & M. G. Shafto (Eds.), *Diagnostic monitoring of skill and knowledge acquisition* (pp. 453–488). Hillsdale, NJ: Lawrence Erlbaum Associates, Inc.

Thorndike, E. L. (1918). Fundamental theorems in judging men. *Journal of Applied Psychology, 2,* 67–76.

Webster, G. D., Shea, J. A., Norcini, J. J., Grosso, L. J., & Swanson, D. B. (1988). Strategies in comparison of methods for scoring patient management problems. *Evaluation and the Health Professions, 11,* 231–248.

Williamson, D. M., Bejar, I. I., & Hone, A. S. (1999). A Mental model comparison of automated and human scoring. *Journal of Educational Measurement, 36,* 158–184.

APPLIED MEASUREMENT IN EDUCATION, *15*(4), 433
Copyright © 2002, Lawrence Erlbaum Associates, Inc.

Guest Reviewers—Volume 15

Manuscripts considered for publication in Volume 15 of *Applied Measurement in Education* were reviewed by the members of the Board of Editors and by the following individuals. The editors thank all the reviewers for their conscientious service to *AME*.

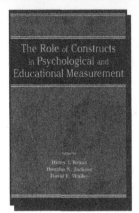

SUBSCRIPTION ORDER FORM

Please ❑ enter ❑ renew my subscription to:

APPLIED MEASUREMENT IN EDUCATION

Volume 16, 2003, Quarterly — ISSN 0895–7347/Online ISSN 1532–4818

SUBSCRIPTION PRICES PER VOLUME:

Category:	Access Type:	Price: US/All Other Countries
❑ Individual	Online & Print	$50.00/$80.00

Subscriptions are entered on a calendar-year basis only and must be paid in advance in U.S. currency—check, credit card, or money order. Prices for subscriptions include postage and handling. **Journal prices expire 12/31/03.** NOTE: Institutions must pay institutional rates. Individual subscription orders are welcome if prepaid by credit card or personal check. **Please note:** A $20.00 penalty will be charged against customers providing checks that must be returned for payment. This assessment will be made only in instances when problems in collecting funds are directly attributable to customer error.

❑   **Check Enclosed** (U.S. Currency Only)   **Total Amount Enclosed $**_____

❑   **Charge My**: ❑ VISA   ❑ MasterCard   ❑ AMEX   ❑ Discover

Card Number _____ Exp. Date____/____

Signature _____
(Credit card orders cannot be processed without your signature.)
PRINT CLEARLY for proper delivery. STREET ADDRESS/SUITE/ROOM # REQUIRED FOR DELIVERY.

Name_____

Address_____

City/State/Zip+4_____

Daytime Phone #_____ E-mail address_____
Prices are subject to change without notice.

For information about online subscriptions, visit our website at *www.erlbaum.com*

Mail orders to: **Lawrence Erlbaum Associates, Inc.,** Journal Subscription Department
10 Industrial Avenue, Mahwah, NJ 07430; **(201) 258–2200; FAX (201) 760–3735; journals@erlbaum.com**

LIBRARY RECOMMENDATION FORM

Detach and forward to your librarian.

❑ I have reviewed the description of *Applied Measurement in Education* and would like to recommend it for acquisition.

APPLIED MEASUREMENT IN EDUCATION

Volume 16, 2003, Quarterly — ISSN 0895–7347/Online ISSN 1532–4818

Category:	Access Type:	Price: US/All Other Countries
❑ Institutional	Online & Print	$420.00/$450.00
❑ Institutional	Online Only	$380.00/$380.00
❑ Institutional	Print Only	$380.00/$410.00

Name_____Title_____

Institution/Department_____

Address_____

E-mail Address_____
Librarians, please send your orders directly to LEA or contact from your subscription agent.

Lawrence Erlbaum Associates, Inc., Journal Subscription Department
10 Industrial Avenue, Mahwah, NJ 07430; **(201) 258–2200; FAX (201) 760–3735; journals@erlbaum.com**

REMAKING THE CONCEPT OF APTITUDE

Extending the Legacy of Richard E. Snow

Lyn Corno, Lee J. Cronbach, Haggai Kupermintz, David F. Lohman, Ellen B. Mandinach, Ann W. Porteus, Joan E. Talbert

for *The Stanford Aptitude Seminar*

Edited by

Lee J. Cronbach

A Volume in the Educational Psychology Series

The unique perspective of Richard E. Snow, in recent years one of the most distinguished educational psychologists, integrates psychology of individual differences, cognitive psychology, and motivational psychology. This capstone book pulls together the findings of his own 35 years of research on aptitudes and those from (especially) European scholars, of which he had exceptional knowledge. A panel of experts and former associates completed this book after his death in 1997, expanding his notes on implications of the theory for instructional design and teaching practice. The panel developed Snow's ideas on where the field should go next, emphasizing promising research strategies.

Viewing intelligence as education's most important product as well as its most important raw material, Snow stressed the need to consider both cognitive skills and affective-motivational characteristics. In this book, previously unconnected research and scattered theoretical ideas are integrated into a dynamic model of aptitude. Understanding the transaction between person and situation was Snow's primary concern. This volume draws from diverse resources to construct a theoretical model of aptitude as a complex process of unfolding person-situation dynamics. *Remaking the Concept of Aptitude: Extending the Legacy of Richard E. Snow*:

* presents historical and contemporary discussion of aptitude theory, illuminating recent ideas by pointing to their historic antecedents;
* provides evidence of how sound research can have practical ramifications in classroom settings;
* discusses the strengths and weaknesses of prominent research programs, including Gardner's "multiple intelligence," meta-analysis, ATI experiments, and information processing;
* describes in detail specific research that has developed important concepts—for example, Czikszentmihalyi on "flow"; Lambrechts on success in stressful training; Sternberg on componential analysis; and Gibson on tailoring affordances to match motivations; and
* keeps statistical complexities to a minimum, and includes a simply written Appendix that explains the interpretation of key technical concepts.

By characterizing sound research in the field, this volume is useful for psychologists and educational researchers. It will also be instructive for teachers seeking to deepen their knowledge of the whole child and for parents of children facing standardized testing.

Contents: Foreword. **R.E. Snow,** Preface. Aptitude: The Once and Future Concept. Conflicting Themes. Mapping the Terrain. Antecedents of Success in Learning. Analyses of Cognitive Process. The Cognitive-Affective-Conative Triad. The Education of Aptitude. Toward a Theory of Aptitude. **Appendix:** Terms Used in Describing Research Studies.
0-8058-3532-6 [cloth] / 2002 / 312pp. / $79.95
Special Discount Price! $34.50
Applies if payment accompanies order or for course adoption orders of 5 or more copies.
No further discounts apply.
Prices are subject to change without notice.

Lawrence Erlbaum Associates, Inc.
10 Industrial Ave., Mahwah, NJ 07430–2262
201–258–2200; 1–800–926–6579; fax 201–760–3735
orders@erlbaum.com; www.erlbaum.com

For Product Safety Concerns and Information please contact our EU representative GPSR@taylorandfrancis.com Taylor & Francis Verlag GmbH, Kaufingerstraße 24, 80331 München, Germany

Printed and bound by CPI Group (UK) Ltd, Croydon, CR0 4YY

01/05/2025

01858513-0001